A Common-Sense Approach to High-Technology Export Controls

John R. Harvey, Cameron Binkley, Adam Block and Rick Burke

A Report of the
Center for International Security
and Arms Control
Stanford University

March 1995

The **Center for International Security and Arms Control,** part of Stanford University's Institute for International Studies, brings together faculty members from several scholarly disciplines with senior specialists from around the world and pre- and postdoctoral fellows for research projects, seminars, conferences, and international scholarly exchange. The Center publishes its own series of reports and papers on its work and also sponsors a series, *Studies in International Security and Arms Control*, through Stanford University Press.

The Center is grateful to the Carnegie Corporation of New York for supporting this publication. The opinions expressed here are those of the authors and do not represent positions of the Center, its supporters, or Stanford University.

Center for International Security and Arms Control
320 Galvez Street
Stanford, California 94305-6165
(415) 723-9625
Douglas Peckler, Editorial Associate

Printed in the United States of America

ISBN 0-935371-35-4

Authors

John R. Harvey is a physicist and Director of the Science Program at the Stanford University Center for International Security and Arms Control (CISAC). Harvey leads research efforts in several areas in which science and technology interrelate with national and international security, including: weapons proliferation in the developing world, U.S. defense restructuring, the implications of advanced conventional weapons technologies for regional security, arms control, and nuclear weapons. He directed the Center's study on high-technology export controls.

Cameron Binkley is a research assistant in the Science Program at CISAC. Binkley's work focuses on weapons proliferation, U.S. export control policy, high-technology manufacturing, and the relationships of these to national and economic security. From 1990 to 1992, he managed the International Missile Proliferation Project at the Monterey Institute of International Studies.

Adam Block, a recent Stanford graduate in political science and international security studies, is currently an operations analyst at *PC World* magazine. From October 1993 to May 1994, he was a CISAC research assistant. Block studied the economic and national security implications of export controls on data encryption products.

Richard P. Burke is an operations research analyst in the Office of the Secretary of Defense (Program Analysis and Evaluation), a position he has held since 1988. For the period September 1992-93, Burke was an International Affairs Fellow of the Council on Foreign Relations. From January through June 1993 he was a visiting research fellow at CISAC. During his stay, his research focused on export control reform in connection with the post-Cold War economic and security environment.

Acknowledgements

The authors are grateful to the following individuals for providing comments and criticism on early drafts of this report, or for otherwise assisting us: Luke Alexander, John Barker, John Barton, Paul Brown, George Bunn, Lew Franklin, Sy Goodman, Richard Gronet, Tom Karas, Lesley Kao, Amos Kovacs, Susan Langford, Maren Leed, Kent McCormick, Mary O'Brien, Brad Roberts, Terry Taylor, and Roszel Thomsen. We thank Elaine Naugle for her research and writing in connection with the Sun Microsystems case study described in Appendix III. We thank Keela Pierce for her research on the role of supercomputers in code breaking. We also appreciate the work of Douglas Peckler, who edited the report into its final form. Finally, we are grateful for the cooperation of those corporations who provided information about the impact of export controls on their organizations. Of course, an individual's willingness to read our drafts, or otherwise offer comment and criticism, should not be construed as an endorsement of the study or its findings.

Part of this work was funded by a grant from the Carnegie Corporation of New York to Stanford University's Center for International Security and Arms Control. The support of the Council on Foreign Relations International Affairs Fellowship Program and the Rockefeller Foundation, which sponsored Dr. Burke's participation in this activity, is also gratefully acknowledged.

Opinions expressed are those of the author(s) and are not necessarily those of the Carnegie Corporation of New York, the Council on Foreign Relations, or the Office of the Secretary of Defense.

Table of Contents

Executive Summary

This report examines the cost and benefits, both national security and economic, of export controls on certain high-technology, dual-use items including computers, microprocessors, commercial aircraft, and methods for data security. We also consider the nature and implications of U.S. unilateral export controls and sanctions, emphasizing the U.S. unilateral embargoes to certain proscribed states, the Enhanced Proliferation Control Initiative (EPCI), and U.S. mandatory sanctions policy under the Missile Technology Control Regime (MTCR). We analyze a few cases in detail rather than offer a generic, and inherently less thorough, review of all dual-use items. Assessments of the utility of high-technology controls cannot be made independently of a detailed analysis of the specific items and destinations subject to controls.

Following is a summary of key findings and conclusions.

High-Technology Trade and International Competition: Implications for Export Controls

Rapid changes in global markets are degrading the effectiveness of export controls on many high-technology products. Corporations have become multinational or international in their R&D, manufacturing, and sales; as a result, many items, including computer and microprocessor design and manufacturing technologies, are being widely disseminated, often to countries not currently participating in any multilateral export control regimes. This diffusion of technology is expanding beyond the traditional reach of Western export controls. More and more developing states are entering high-technology manufacturing industries specifically to generate export earnings to finance domestic economic development. This trend will inevitably generate new sources, and new markets, for high-technology items, and new competitors for U.S. firms.

In these fiercely competitive markets, export controls have real economic costs with direct and indirect effects on U.S. firms. First, firms directly lose some sales from denied exports licenses. Second, long delays in acquiring licenses have killed some deals. Onerous end-use safeguards on computers have increased their cost, making U.S. firms less competitive in some markets. U.S. controls on re-exports give foreign manufacturers incentives to "design out" U.S.-made components used in their products. The need to retain staff experts in the specialized field of export controls increases a firm's administrative costs; small firms are often deterred from exporting their products precisely for this reason. Denied exports create incentives for states to develop a home-grown capability for producing needed items; U.S. export controls thus can give rise to new competitors to U.S. firms. Finally, with military industry increasingly "piggybacking" off civilian technological innovation, export controls can narrow existing U.S. advantages in defense capability if, by closing markets, they constrain commercial re-investment in R&D.

Export Controls on High-Performance Computers

Contrary to the conventional wisdom, high-performance computers are not an enabling technology for nuclear weapons; export controls on these systems will thus have little relevance in restraining nuclear proliferation. Building a few relatively unsophisticated weapons requires only modest calculational capability, at the level of personal computers two or more generations old and now widely available.

Supercomputers of the very highest performance levels are where the key leverage resides for the United States in keeping its technological lead in such areas as advanced conventional weapons (including stealth) and cryptography. Moreover, these systems are more controllable because there are currently only two supplier countries—the United States and Japan—and they often agree on the undesirable end-users. Alternatively, there is little value in trying to control computers at lower performance levels; these systems are much less useful in advanced conventional weapons design or in cryptography. Export controls should, therefore, focus on maintaining our technological lead in "true" supercomputers without affecting sales of less powerful systems.

Special, massively parallel, hybrid computers are relevant for code breaking; export controls should emphasize the special microprocessors peculiar to the specific encryption algorithms used in these systems.

Export Controls on Microprocessors

The wide availability of microprocessors, coupled with their small size and volume sales, has undermined effective export control, and for this reason the United States began to relax controls on these items in the mid-1980s. Today, U.S. microprocessor exports are virtually unrestricted except to a handful of states. But the relaxation of microprocessor export controls has, in certain cases, actually harmed the U.S. computer industry, particularly in the personal computer and workstation market sectors. This is because the decontrol of advanced microprocessors has outpaced the decontrol of the computer platforms based on these microprocessors. As a result, some computer firms, especially in newly industrialized states, have been able to use U.S. microprocessors in the design and manufacture of computer clones that they then market in competition with platforms of equivalent performance sold by U.S. firms.

Until recently, however, the competition was not on a "level playing field." For example, foreign-made clones were often exported to countries, including the former CoCom targets, where U.S. computers of comparable performance were denied entry. In addition, foreign firms gained advantage by being able to sell immediately to certain destinations where U.S. firms experienced significant licensing delays. In both cases U.S. firms were placed at a competitive disadvantage because of the disparity between microprocessor and computer controls.

The recent relaxation of computer controls has eased the problem for the time being. But the pace of technological progress is so rapid that microprocessors now in development will, as soon as they are released, exceed, or come close to exceeding, today's performance thresholds for computer export controls. When this occurs U.S. exporters will be at a competitive disadvantage until thresholds are raised once again. A balance can be struck by routinely raising the control threshold on computer performance as each new generation of microprocessors is introduced, making controls more responsive to the pace of technology.

Export Controls on Mass-Market Encryption Software

The United States strictly controls exports of encryption products, including mass-market software with strong encryption capability, because of concerns that potential foes could take advantage of this software to communicate over global networks free from eavesdropping. The software industry has sought to relax controls on encryption products, arguing that many public domain encryption algorithms are uncontrollable.

Strong encryption algorithms and associated software are indeed in the public domain, but these technologies have not been put to widespread use globally. As a result, they seem to have not yet created insurmountable problems for U.S. intelligence. This could change if U.S.-produced mass-market business software embedded with strong encryption becomes widely available overseas. It would result in an explosive increase in encrypted message traffic, decreasing the Intelligence Community's ability to perform broad keyword searches and taxing the capacity of computers used in decoding. There appears to be a strong case this would harm national security.

But national security arguments do not necessarily override the software industry's case. U.S. firms and their overseas subsidiaries, partners, customers, and competitors rely a great deal on modern telecommunications and this reliance is likely to grow in the future. Because information security will be important for engaging these markets, and because the global and widespread use of encryption seems inevitable, the longer such use is blocked by concerns over intelligence-gathering complications, the greater the potential harm to U.S. economic interests. Indeed, if U.S. firms are unable to assure the privacy of communications with overseas entities, they become increasingly vulnerable to industrial espionage, which has a very high cost.

In trying to reconcile the competing interests, we urge a "go-slow" approach to export control reform in this area. While controls should continue for the time being, an independent study of national cryptography policy should assess the national security implications of a phased decontrol of software products with encryption. U.S. business interests can be better factored into licensing decisions by making the Commerce Department the lead agency for controlling all mass-market encryption software. U.S. firms should be given greater flexibility to use strong encryption products in overseas business activities. Finally, R&D funding to the National Security Agency must be at a sufficient level to permit development of new technologies and methods to mitigate the effects of the inevitable increased use of strong encryption in routine telecommunications.

U.S. Unilateral Controls and Their Implications

U.S. companies often must compete under rules that do not apply to their foreign competitors. Examples are the unilateral export controls and sanctions the United States imposes on several states, or entities within states, mainly in support of non-proliferation and anti-terrorism. These often prevent exports of commercial items having no military value at all and are unpopular within the U.S. business community.

If the United States is a sole supplier of particular items, then unilateral controls could be an effective denial strategy. But what if the target state can acquire equivalent products, both in quality and quantity, from other sources willing to sell? In this case, there is little benefit to offset the economic cost in lost sales to U.S. companies. Alternatively, some argue that even in the presence of widespread foreign availability, unilateral export controls can play an important role in attaining critical U.S. foreign policy goals. Even if ineffective in denying trade to targeted states, they are symbolic of the principled stands that the United States may take as a leader in world affairs. They also may act to highlight the undesirable behavior of a target state in the eyes of the international community. By conveying resolve, unilateral controls influence others to cooperate with the United States in seeking the improved behavior of a target state.

In trying to assess these conflicting arguments we analyzed three cases involving unilateral controls: the Iran embargo and its impact on U.S. sales of commercial airliners, the "catch-all" provision of the Enhanced Proliferation Control Initiative, and U.S. sanctions policy under the MTCR. In each instance, we find that U.S. policies on balance are counterproductive to overall U.S. economic and foreign policy interests. Generally, the United States should not impose unilateral controls on commercial items for which it is not the sole supplier. If other key suppliers do not go along with them, controls will be both ineffective and costly to U.S. firms. If imposed for overriding political reasons, unilateral controls should be accompanied with "sunset provisions" that go into effect after a fixed period of time unless the controls have become multilateral. In this connection, substantive reviews of U.S. unilateral controls should be conducted semi-annually. The EPCI "catch-all" rule should be substantially revised or, failing that, eliminated, and the President should be given more discretion in imposing sanctions under the MTCR. More generally, the President should have the flexibility to allow or, alternatively, ban specific exports to specific end-users when dictated by overriding national security or economic interests.

Detailed conclusions and recommendations from our study may be found in Section VII.

I. Introduction

President Clinton's stunning announcements over the past two years slashing export controls on high-performance computers have set the stage for a major policy review of the post-Cold War role of export controls on high technology.[1] The President concluded that the economic costs resulting from restrictive export controls outweighed the national security benefits. This decision did not come alone; he has also eased controls on advanced telecommunications technologies and, as part of his strategy to lessen the burden for U.S. industry, restrictions on transfers or sales of space launch systems and technologies to certain destinations.[2] Perhaps more so than any preceding ones, the export promotion and control policies of this administration reflect a strong appreciation of the link between economic security and national security.

Critics charge that the President and his Secretary of Defense have declared war on export controls, opening the floodgates on key technologies to states proliferating weapons of mass destruction (WMD).[3] Although most of the criticism is unwarranted, the debate raises a central question: How can export controls enhance U.S. security in the post Cold-War era without unduly harming the competitiveness of U.S. firms? This question is the central focus of our study.

U.S. National Security Strategy and the Role of Export Controls

In the post-Cold War era, the United States faces four major security threats: (1) the proliferation of weapons of mass destruction, (2) the threat of regional conflict, (3) the potential for a resurgent, hostile superpower emerging from the former Soviet Union, and (4) threats to economic interests. These threats could occur as direct threats to the continental United States, as threats to allies and U.S. forces deployed overseas, or as threats to regional security and stability that could involve the United States.

With the Cold War's end, the likelihood of superpower military confrontation has receded and with it the most significant threat to U.S. security—the devastation from thermonuclear war. Indeed, states that might wish to attack the United States with nuclear weapons do not yet have that capability, and states having the capability (e.g., the former Soviet Union and China) may no longer have the intent. Today, threats to the United States are much less predictable than superpower conflict, and wars would be much less devastating. At the same time, conflict at a lower level may be more likely to occur.

If the major nuclear threat to the United States has been all but eliminated, why should one care about nuclear weapons that do not directly threaten the United States? There are three main reasons. First, there is the humanitarian concern that these weapons could kill many people, including U.S. allies, even if they do not kill Americans. Second, the acquisition (or use) of nuclear weapons could increase regional instabilities in a way that could draw the United States into conflicts. Finally, and perhaps most significantly for U.S. security policy, nuclear weapons or other WMDs in the hands of an otherwise inferior adversary act as force "equalizers," which can deny the United States the freedom of action to intervene in particular regions as may be warranted. The question is always asked: What if Iraq had possessed the bomb?

The United States will thus continue to deploy a survivable, residual nuclear deterrent as a hedge against a potential resurgent threat from the FSU, China, and emerging nuclear weapons states. Further, it will be essential to deter and, if necessary, defeat conventional or nuclear aggression, preferably with conventional forces, in areas of the world where critical interests, as determined by the President and Congress, are at stake. To achieve this, sufficient conventional military forces must be fielded and, most importantly, these forces must be qualitatively superior. At the same time, the United States must work with its international partners to restrain the proliferation of WMD and advanced conventional military technologies to potential adversaries.

It is on this last point where export controls on WMD-related technologies and other critical defense technologies continue to play a role in U.S. security policy. Export controls, however, will be but one arrow in the policy quiver, which includes strengthened global non-proliferation norms, attention to regional security cooperation and guarantees, and a U.S. military capability well-suited to deter conflict in the post-Cold War period. For reasons addressed in this report, the effectiveness of export controls, and hence their role in U.S. security policy, will inevitably decline with time.

Background

Export controls have long been an integral part of Western multilateral security arrangements. Their purpose has been to support alliance foreign and defense policies by denying potential adversaries the military and commercial benefits of trade with the West. Soon after World War II the West, faced with the threat of Soviet expansionism, moved quickly to restrict trade with the Eastern bloc. It was understood that quantitatively superior Warsaw Pact forces could be countered either by fielding numerically equivalent Western military forces or by seeking technological superiority in quantitatively fewer forces. The political and economic advantages of the latter strategy prevailed upon leaders of the newly formed NATO, and, in 1949, its members established the Coordinating Committee for Multilateral Export Controls—CoCom—a system to regulate East-West trade.[4] CoCom was designed to help secure and advance the West's qualitative military edge by preventing Soviet access to both commercial and defense-related high-technology products, services, and manufacturing know-how.

CoCom is generally considered a success because nearly all of the principal suppliers of key products and technologies participated in restricting access to the Soviet Union. But the multilateral consensus to form CoCom was driven by the immediacy of the Soviet threat. Today, with the collapse of Soviet power, the widespread adoption of democracy and free market institutions in the formerly communist states, and the rising importance of high technology trade in an increasingly competitive global economy, that consensus has come apart. Indeed, as a result of these trends, CoCom was "disestablished" by its members on April 1, 1994.

In its place a "New Forum" has been proposed: a technology export control regime to be established in response to concerns about the proliferation of WMD and advanced conventional military technologies to unstable regions of the world. This New Forum would not be targeted against Russia, but would include Russia and other Eastern European states as founding members. Indeed, it would be open to all countries willing to (1) endorse non-proliferation norms, (2) adhere to existing export control regimes other than CoCom, and (3) implement effective domestic export control systems. The targets of the new regime would be states not adhering to non-proliferation norms or otherwise exhibiting undesirable behavior.

It is unlikely that the threat of WMD proliferation will galvanize the industrial states to implement stringent export controls to the same degree that the Soviet threat did.[5] Thus, the New Forum is likely to be considerably weaker than CoCom in many respects. For example, licensing decisions under the New Forum will be based on "national discretion," rather than the CoCom "consensus" rule under which any member could block a proposed export by another member to a targeted state. The United States, however, is pressing for a rule in which the parties would be required to give prior notification of exports intended for a narrowly targeted group of states. Though not a veto, this would allow opposing governments the opportunity to voice concerns before a potentially undesirable export occurs.

At the time of this writing the New Forum has not yet been established and thus we cannot provide a more comprehensive analysis of its structure or operation. Still, it is timely to reassess the role of dual-use export controls in view of the geopolitical and global economic trends deriving from the end of the Cold War. Indeed, this process is already underway in the United States as evidenced by the Congressional debate in 1994 on export control reform legislation. (For an overview of the U.S. export control system, see Appendix I.)

Recent Work

In 1987, the National Academy of Sciences (NAS) Committee on Science, Engineering, and Public Policy published a major report calling for reform in U.S. export control policies.[6] Among other things, the committee urged that the United States seek to balance its economic interests and national security interests in the consideration, adoption, and implementation of export controls on dual-use technology. Further, it found that controls, in order to be effective, should be multilateral. A related study identified several major trends bearing on the utility and effectiveness of export controls in the specific area of computer technology.[7] These trends included: the rapid advances in computer technologies, the globalization of computer and computer-related industry, the fact that computers and associated components were becoming commodity products, and the easing of East-West tensions then underway that reduced the need to control computer technology as stringently as before.

By 1988, partly in response to this relaxation in tensions, Congress called for a second NAS review on the state of U.S. national security export controls and their effect on three important sectors of U.S. industry: advanced industrial materials, commercial aircraft and jet engines, and computer technology. The landmark study, *Finding Common Ground,* was published in 1991 and called for further significant reforms.[8] A key finding urged that CoCom be transformed from a "denial regime" to an "approval regime" whereby exports would be allowed if certain criteria were met. The study addressed the increasing importance of export controls in impeding the proliferation of weapons of mass destruction, and the need to engage the Soviet Union and China in order to make such controls effective. It recommended that non-proliferation controls be narrowly focused in the areas of highest risk to avoid harming unnecessarily other U.S. commercial and foreign policy interests.

Following the collapse of the Soviet Union, a NAS workshop, initiated on the basis of this previous work, was commissioned to study remaining East-West security concerns and the role of export controls, as well as the relationship of such controls to non-proliferation.[9] Participants reached consensus on several broad themes including the rise of new post-Cold War security threats, the need for the United States to develop a new national security strategy (the absence of which makes export control policy difficult to formulate), the need to define more carefully the technologies to be controlled, and the need to reach agreement on redefining CoCom in order to keep it relevant in the post-Cold War period. Further, it was concluded that export controls should continue to have a strong multilateral component.

In May 1994, the U.S. Congress's Office of Technology Assessment (OTA) published a comprehensive study of the emerging relationship between export controls and non-proliferation policy.[10] The OTA report developed options for enhancing export control effectiveness (e.g., by strengthening multilateral arrangements) and easing the burdens on U.S. companies. Among other things, it emphasized the importance of keeping separate the export regimes for controlling conventional weapons and associated technologies (formerly coordinated in CoCom) from those controlling the proliferation of weapons of mass destruction. Because no consensus exists among states for controlling conventional arms transfers, OTA argued that combining regimes risks weakening the strong consensus on controls to impede WMD proliferation. OTA also found that considerations of U.S. economic interests should be factored into the implementation of non-proliferation export controls.[11]

Scope and Organization of the Present Study

Our study has been influenced by, and builds on, this substantial body of previous work. During 1993 we conducted a series of interviews with officials from industry, government, and academia conversant with the complex issues concerning high-technology export controls. In October 1993, a two-day workshop on export controls was held at Stanford University, which included as participants many of those interviewed, and other outside experts.[12] Some of the ideas discussed herein were first raised at the Stanford workshop.

Our focus has been the cost and benefits, both national security and economic, of export controls on certain high-technology, dual-use items including computers, microprocessors, commercial aircraft, and methods for data security. We analyze a few cases in detail rather than offer a generic, and inherently less thorough, review of the items on the Commerce Control List.[13] By doing this, we hope to convince the reader that general comments about the utility of high-technology controls really cannot be made independently of a detailed analysis of the specific items subject to controls. Indeed, for export controls the "devil is in the details."

Thus, our comments on the utility (or lack thereof) of controls on particular items are offered in the specific context of the cases studied. For example, our conclusion that controls on high-performance computers are ineffective in constraining a state's ability to develop first-generation nuclear weapons, should not be generalized to mean that we oppose controls on other items, including many of those on the Nuclear Supplier's List, which do indeed act to impede nuclear proliferation. With the exception of encryption software, the study does not address controls on items listed in the State Department's International Traffic in Arms Regulations (ITAR), which are either munitions or principally defense-related and often have few, if any, commercial applications.

This report is organized as follows: In Section II, we describe the nature of the global market in high-technology products, its importance to the United States, and its implications for export controls on high technology. We address why export controls are destined, over time, to become less and less effective and assess the general impact of controls on the competitiveness of many high-technology firms. In Section III, we evaluate the utility of export controls on high-performance computers in three areas that impact on U.S. security: the design, development, and manufacture of nuclear weapons by proliferant states; maintaining a technological lead in advanced conventional weapons; and cryptography. Section IV addresses the specific question of export controls on microprocessors—a key component in modern computers. In Section V, we identify issues associated with continued controls on means to secure computer telecommunications, specifically mass-market software products with encryption capability. Section VI examines the nature and implications of U.S. unilateral controls and sanctions—the focus is on U.S. unilateral embargoes to certain proscribed states, the enhanced proliferation control initiative (EPCI), and U.S. mandatory sanctions policy under the Missile Technology Control Regime (MTCR). Section VII offers conclusions and recommendations.

A Note on the Costs of Export Controls to U.S. Firms

In this study we tried to obtain hard data on the actual financial costs of export controls to U.S. high-technology firms. Such data is not readily available except in certain instances such as the Boeing-Iran Air case described in Section VI.[14] Although we understand that denied export licenses are not a particularly useful gauge of overall export-control related costs, other widely reported figures have often turned out to be based on false assumptions or speculation. Many company officials interviewed for this study either have not developed the numbers for their export control-related costs, or are unwilling to divulge them. Part of the problem is the inherent difficulty in estimating "lost business" resulting from controls. A complicating factor is that corporate accounting techniques often intertwine the administrative costs of export controls with other overhead expenses. A recent important book by J. David Richardson, referred to in Section II, uses macroeconomic analysis to provide a broad range of estimates of the costs of export controls to U.S. firms.[15] These costs derive mainly from denied markets in the former Soviet bloc. Richardson, however, does not break down cost data by major industrial sector and, thus, we are unable to apply his work to specific cases addressed in this study.

II. High-Technology Trade And Competition In International Markets

In this section, we examine the relationship of high-technology industries and international export markets to the U.S. economy and assess implications for future export control policies. We conclude that the strength of U.S. firms in high-technology sectors is becoming increasingly dependent on the ability of firms to participate and compete vigorously in global markets. The following issues are considered:

- What are the high-technology industries and why are they important to the United States?
- Why are a growing number of countries pursuing these industries?
- What global changes are occurring in the factors of production for high-technology industries?
- How do economies of scale, scope, and learning influence the international competition for global market share in high-technology industries?
- How do industrial performance and employment trends in the industrialized states influence the international competition for market shares in high-technology goods and services?
- What are the implications for U.S. export control policies in the post Cold-War period?

The High-Technology Industries

High-technology industries are, in general, ones in which knowledge is the primary source of comparative advantage for producers of goods and services. Firms in high-technology sectors make large investments in the creation of knowledge and intellectual property that form the basis for their products and services. As shown in Tables 1 and 2, these industries generally have above average spending on research and development (R&D), and employ more scientists and engineers than the average for all manufacturing sectors.

Several classification schemes have been developed to identify and group high-technology industries for the purpose of measuring and comparing economic performance and output. One of the simplest, developed by the Organization for Economic Cooperation and Development (OECD), identifies six industrial sectors as the high-technology industries: (1) drugs and medicines, (2) office machinery and computers, (3) electrical machinery, (4) electronic components (and communications), (5) aerospace, and (6) scientific instruments.[1] It is of note that each of these industrial categories is dual-use in nature—having both civilian and military applications.

High-Technology Industries in the U.S. Economy

High-technology industries are important contributors to the U.S. manufacturing base. Together the high-technology industrial sectors account for approximately 20% of manufacturing output in the United States, and about 1/4 of the value-added in the manufacturing sector. Approximately 60% of the industrial R&D in the United States is performed within high-technology industrial categories. Two of the high-technology sectors—the electronics complex (computers and office equipment, communications, electronic components, and audio and video equipment) and the aerospace complex (aircraft and missiles)—accounted for about 2/3 of the total R&D spending by U.S. high-technology industries in 1989.[2]

A key characteristic of high-technology industries is the high-productivity, high-wage employment provided in these industrial sectors. In the United States, the value added per worker in the high-technology industries is approximately 1/3 larger than the average for workers in all manufacturing sectors. For production workers alone, the value added per worker in the high-tech industries is about 2/3 higher than the average for all manufacturing sectors.[3]

The high-productivity of these workers is reflected in relatively high wages paid in these industries. The average compensation for U.S. high-technology industry workers is approximately 22% higher than the

Industry	Industry R&D Funding (millions of dollars)[1]	Share of Total R&D expenditures by all manufacturing firms
Industrial Organic Chemicals[2]	3,972	5.7 %
Drugs	5,206	7.4%
Computers and office equipment	10,533	15.0%
Audio and video equipment	85	0.1%
Communications equipment	5,842	8.3%
Electronics components, and accessories	4,362	6.2%
Aircraft and missiles	6,020	8.6%
Scientific instruments[3]	5,638	8.0%
All high-technology industries	41,658	59.3%
All industries	70,233	100.0%
High-technology share of total R&D (percent)[4]	59%	

Table 1 United States: high-technology expenditures for R&D, by industry 1989 (Source: Tyson, 1992: Data supplied by the National Science Foundation)

1 Funds from all sources except the federal government.

2 Includes SICs 281 (inorganic chemicals) 282 (plastics) and 286 (organic chemicals) rather than only the two high-technology categories (281 and 282).

3 Includes SIC 3825 (electrical test and measurement instruments).

4 These estimates understate the actual share because ordnance and engines are excluded from the high-technology total but included in the all-industries total.

Industry	Scientists and engineers per 1000 employees	Ratio to average for manufacturing	Imputed number of scientists and engineers	Percentage of total for all U.S. firms
Industrial Organic Chemicals[a]	53	1.18	18,115	2%
Drugs	97	2.16	16,674	2%
Ordinance and accessories	n.a.	n.a.	n.a.	n.a.
Engines and turbines	n.a.	n.a.	n.a.	n.a.
Computers and office equipment	113	2.51	37,030	4%
Audio and video equipment	44	.98	1,945	< 1%
Communications equipment	72	1.60	18,734	2%
Electronics components and accessories	90	2.00	49,176	6%
Aircraft and missiles	89	1.98	72,063	8%
Scientific instruments[b]	75	1.67	73,680	9%
Average for all high-technology industries[c]	82	1.83	287,418	34%
Average for all manufacturing	45	1.00	852,764	100%

Table 2 United States: scientists and engineers employed in selected high-technology industries, 1989. (Source: Tyson, 1992: National Science Foundation, *Research and Development in Industry*, 1989.)

n.a. = not available (for some industries, data are withheld by the National Science Foundation to avoid disclosing the operations of individual companies).

[a] Includes SICs 281 (inorganic chemicals) 282 (plastics) and 286 (organic chemicals) rather than only the two high-technology categories (281 and 282).

[b] Includes SIC 3825 (electrical test and measurement instruments).

[c] Calculated as the weighted average of all categories in table except ordnance and ammunition, and engines and turbines, using total industry employment as weights. The imputed number of scientists and engineers for all high-technology industry is the sum for the individual industries.

average for all manufacturing workers; the wages for production workers are about 15% higher than the average for production workers in all manufacturing sectors.[4]

Because of the complex interdependence of the U.S. industrial structure, high-technology industries stimulate productivity improvements in seemingly unrelated industrial sectors. For example, the U.S. textile industry—considered by many to be a low-technology industrial sector—has significantly increased its productivity by incorporating advanced manufacturing equipment and processing technologies created in the high-tech industrial sectors.[5]

High-Technology Industries and International Economic Development

High-technology industries are becoming an increasingly important part of the productive capabilities of countries at all levels of economic development. This has been brought about by the continuing liberalization of trade and investment in the worldwide economy—an evolving process that began following World War II with the start of the international trading system at Bretton Woods. The growth in world-wide trade has recently accelerated with the conclusion of international negotiations on trade agreements such as the North American Free Trade Agreement and the General Agreement on Tariffs and Trade.

States pursuing the benefits of high-technology industries now span the economic spectrum from the developing countries of the Third World to the advanced, industrialized societies of Europe, Asia, and North America. A growing number of countries seek to emulate the "Asian model" of economic development—best demonstrated by Japan after World War II—in which technology goods are exported and sold on international markets to finance domestic economic development and industrialization. This model has been employed in varying degrees in a growing number of the newly industrialized states—most notably Singapore, Taiwan, and South Korea—to successfully replace more traditional economic development programs involving extensive capital financing which led many states heavily into debt.

The high-technology industries have other characteristics that make them attractive in the emerging era of economic globalization. The relatively high productivity and high wages of employees in these sectors provide tremendous advantages to the local economies in which the firms operate. As a result, governments have consistently demonstrated a willingness to finance incentive packages to attract these industries. For example, in 1993 New Mexico offered an incentive package worth approximately $114 million to entice Intel Corporation to construct a large semiconductor fabrication plant at Rio Rancho, which will directly employ approximately 1,000 people.[6] Recently, the governments of China, Vietnam, and the countries of the Association of Southeast Asian Nations (ASEAN) have been attracting technology industries through generous incentives, such as special tax privileges, offered in "special economic zones."[7]

Trends and Changes in Availability of Factors of Production

The essential factors of production for high-technology industries—financial capital, skilled labor, and advanced technologies—are increasingly available and mobile in global markets. These factors of production, unlike those for traditional smokestack industries, may be acquired or created through domestic policies and do not depend on extensive endowments of natural resources.

The availability of the factors of production for technology industries makes it possible for many countries to join in the international competition for the benefits of high-technology industries, including high-productivity employment, high-wage rates, and local economic "spillover" benefits.[8] For example, Malaysia, a developing country, has developed its "Vision 2020" plan with the explicit objective of achieving the status of a fully industrialized state by the year 2020. To achieve this objective the Malaysian government is executing a plan for expansion of the existing base of technology firms—including more than 70 multinational and international firms in the electronics sector—already operating in the region near Kuala Lumpur. The high growth rates of all of the newly industrialized economies in the past 25 years is partly attributed to their success in attracting and building niches in the high-technology industrial sectors.

Financial Capital. Several important trends in worldwide financial markets have improved access to financial capital for creation of high-technology industry, with direct effects on global economic competition. One of these is the marked increase in foreign direct investment (FDI) that has resulted from continuing economic liberalization throughout the world. More and more, states are using economic free zones, government subsidies, reduced taxes, and low-interest loans to attract FDI from high-technology firms. Firms are benefiting—foreign investment has become for them a key vehicle to develop new, high-growth international markets for high-technology products. For example, from 1983 to 1990, worldwide FDI outflows increased at the unprecedented rate of 29% per year, three times faster than the world growth of exports and four times faster than the growth of world output during this period.[9] In 1990 the total world FDI outflow rose to a level of $196 billion. The collapse of the Warsaw Pact and the end of the Cold War has increased substantially the amount of foreign investment flowing into Eastern Europe. FDI—along with free trade among countries—is becoming a principal means of international economic integration in the post-Cold War era.[10]

Skilled Work Force. Developing countries are increasingly choosing to make investments in education and training to acquire skilled workers for design, development, and manufacturing of high-technology products. Advanced telecommunication and information technologies now make it possible and affordable to train workers at remote sites throughout the world.

Advanced Technologies. The rate of diffusion of technologies in the world is accelerating as a result of the growing number of multinational and international firms, international joint ventures, transnational R&D projects, international conferences and publications, and the global licensing of intellectual property. In addition, the scale intensities of technology industries require firms to seek out new markets for goods wherever they may be—even in small and developing countries—increasing the diffusion of technologies throughout the world. For example, several of the Silicon Valley firms examined during the course of this study do business in more than 100 countries.

The increasing availability of the factors of production in world markets makes it possible for a broad spectrum of countries to become players and create niches in international markets for high-technology products. This process is creating new markets—as well as new competitors—for U.S. firms in the high-technology sectors.

Scale Economies and Competition in International Markets

The economics of high-technology industries strongly favor the advantages of large-scale production. The industries generally demonstrate strong economies of scale, scope, and learning.

Economies of Scale. High-technology firms invest substantial financial resources in R&D to create knowledge and intellectual property that forms the basis for their products and services. These R&D costs must be recovered in revenues from the sales of products and services in international markets. Firms that increase their global market share acquire a larger sales base for recovery of R&D costs and reduce product costs to achieve pricing advantages over competitors. Thus, high-technology firms are driven to gain the largest international market shares possible to gain structural pricing advantages over competitors or later entrants to markets.

Economies of Scope. The production of multiple products in the same business line provides a mechanism for achieving economies in many high-technology industries. For example, the design and production of a complete line of commercial aircraft results in economies of scope as common parts and components are incorporated into different models.

Economies of Learning. The technological know-how and the effects of learning-by-doing result in a decrease in unit production costs with increasing production in nearly all manufacturing industries, including the high-technology sectors.

The strong scale intensities for high-technology industries are fueling a fierce international competition for global market share in a number of industrial sectors. Firms are driven to export to the greatest degree possible to achieve cost and pricing advantages over global competitors or potential new market entrants. Indeed, large U.S. high-technology firms typically derive more than half of their revenues from export sales. As a result, many high-technology firms are becoming world leaders in economic integration through export trade.

Employment in Industrialized Nations and International Competition

Recently a number of advanced industrialized states, most notably certain Western European countries and Japan, have experienced problems with negative trends in employment. For example, the 1993 unemployment rate for the European Union (EU) countries averaged approximately 12%—five times higher than the unemployment rate of three decades ago.[11] Similar trends have been exhibited to a lesser degree in Japan. Known for the lowest unemployment in the industrialized world for several decades, Japan is now struggling to cope with unemployment rates between 2 and 3%. Some Japanese firms are struggling to maintain their commitment to lifetime employment for workers.[12]

A portion of the unemployment in industrialized states can be explained by a worldwide surplus of labor, which is related to the growing liberalization of trade and investment policies throughout the world. Indeed, as a result of this liberalization, many developing countries are now capable of manufacturing high-quality products at low cost—products that are in demand in global markets. Unfortunately, unemployment may persist at higher than desirable levels in several industrialized states for the foreseeable future—despite actions taken by industrialized states to improve productivity and spur economic growth.

Higher than desirable unemployment in industrialized states is likely to intensify the international competition for high-technology industries—a key source of high-productive, high-wage jobs. Economic growth in the developing world is expected to exceed that of the industrialized states during the next decade. Therefore, high-technology firms must enter these expanding markets as a means of increasing revenues, especially as growth remains sluggish in the industrialized states. Markets in developing countries are also generally less crowded and less saturated with high-technology goods than those in the industrialized states. Trade frictions in high-technology sectors are expected to continue in the industrialized states, and may also extend to developing countries that achieve success in the international markets for technology products.

Implications for Export Controls

The rapid changes in global markets are degrading the effectiveness of export controls on many high-technology products. Corporations have become multinational or international in their R&D, manufacturing, and sales; as a result, many items, including computer and microprocessor design and manufacturing technologies, are being widely disseminated, often to countries not currently participating in any multilateral export control regimes. Thus, technology is not only diffusing, but its spread is expanding beyond the traditional reach of Western export controls. As discussed, more and more developing states are entering high-technology manufacturing industries specifically to generate export earnings to finance domestic economic development. As states continue to pursue this Asian model of development, the process will inevitably generate new sources and new markets for high-technology items, and new competitors for U.S. firms.[13]

Economies of scale, scope, and learning result in strong scale intensities for high-technology industries, and thus firms that are first to introduce products gain significant "first mover" advantages over later entrants.[14] Structural impediments, such as export controls, that delay or prevent the entry of firms into international markets will generally reduce first mover advantages, reduce market share, and result in lower profits for firms—particularly considering the short product life cycles characteristic of high-technology industries.

Consider, for example, the global market in computer hardware. The price, performance, and availability of computers has changed dramatically in recent years. Today, personal computers with performance equal to mainframes of only ten years ago are becoming basic commodities, available off-the-shelf from numerous world-wide sources at relatively low prices. Where once there existed only a limited product line from a few companies, now a variety of comparable products covering the entire performance spectrum is available.[15] Today the largest producer of personal computers is not the United States, but Taiwan. Taiwanese firms, largely unhampered by export controls, tend to be only 120 days behind U.S. manufacturers in introducing the latest product lines.

As indicated in Table 3, the global computer market generates revenues of about $100 billion a year divided over five product segments characterized by a rough performance level or range. The industry is still highly lucrative for U.S. firms, which currently capture about 60% of total market share but do so by dominating the high end in workstations and supercomputers. Each product segment area is highly competitive and first-to-market advantages are critical, particularly when marketing windows are on the order of a year to 18 months. Not only are these markets fiercely competitive, but the technologies develop so fast that it is hard for professionals to keep up, including government officials involved with export controls.[16] Similar trends are observed in other high-technology sectors.

In such an environment, export controls have real economic costs with direct and indirect effects on U.S. firms. First, firms directly lose some sales—generally considered to be small—from denied export licenses.[17] Second, long delays in acquiring licenses have killed some deals. Also, onerous end-use safeguards on computers have increased their cost, making U.S. firms less competitive for certain international deals. U.S. controls on re-exports give foreign manufacturers incentives to "design out" U.S.-made components used in their products. Finally, the need to retain staff experts in the specialized field of export controls increases a firm's administrative costs; small firms are often deterred from exporting their products precisely for this reason.

Denied exports may also create incentives for states to develop a homegrown capability for producing needed items; U.S. export controls can thus give birth to new competitors to its own firms. In deciding whether to site new plants here or abroad, or whether to invest in or form partnerships with foreign firms, U.S. firms consider several factors including political stability, labor costs, capital availability, and government regulations including export controls. In weighing such decisions disparate export control regulations may be decisive in swaying the outcome.[18]

In his landmark study, economist J. David Richardson uses a complex statistical approach combined with "forensic" analysis to calculate the costs of "demand-constricting" U.S. "export disincentives" (which are largely export controls).[19] Based upon his analysis and using data collected for 1989 and 1991, Richardson estimates that the overall annual cost to the United States of national security export controls is from $1.7-$19.9 billion and that similar foreign policy export controls cost from $2.4-$3.1 billion. Indeed, after substantial liberalization, the burden of export controls grew in 1991 because the volume of high-technology exports (the sector most largely affected by export controls) grew even further. Richardson concludes that the likely response of some enterprising U.S.

Computer	World Revenue	Revenue of U.S. Firms	Market Share of U.S. Firms	R&D Spending of U.S. Firms
PC (10-50 Mflop)	$46.5 B	$25 B	54%	$0.75 B
Workstations (50-500 Mflop)	$9.0 B	$8.0 B	89%	$0.80 B
Midrange (100-1000 Mflop)	$24.7 B	$14.1 B	57%	$0.80 B
Mainframe (2-10 Gflop)	$22.5 B	$13.0 B	58%	$2.0 B
Supercomputer (> 10 Gflop)	$1.8 B	$1.3 B	72%	$0.20 B
Total	$104.5 B	$61.4 B	59%	$4.6 B

Table 3: The worldwide market for computer hardware. The figures are for 1992. The R&D spending by U.S. firms amounted to about $4.6 billion for 1992. For comparison, ARPA's program for massively parallel processors (MPP) was funded that year at a level of about $0.4 billion, and the HPCCI initiative at about $1.0 billion. A megaflop (Mflop) is one million floating point operations per second. (1000 Mflop = 1 Gflop.) The performance levels cited are only notional.

multinational firms has been to transfer operations abroad. Although U.S. multinationals held a stable 17-18% of world export market share for two decades, the share of U.S.-domiciled parent firms slipped from 10.7% in 1966 to 8.1% in 1988 with the slack being transferred off-shore, to majority-held U.S. affiliates (from 6.6% in 1966 to 8.9% in 1988).[20]

Export controls not only have economic costs but they can, in certain cases, be counterproductive from the national security perspective. As military budgets have declined, DoD is no longer the principal agent driving many technological advances. Increasingly, the defense sector is "piggybacking" on commercial technology sectors, which are becoming more global and more widely available to potential adversaries. Thus, U.S. commercial high-technology industries must continue to generate advances in critical dual-use technologies, and DoD must upgrade military hardware to exploit these advances before others do. To the degree that export controls hinder U.S. high-technology firms from competing in global markets, fewer revenues and profits will be available for reinvestment in R&D, critical technologies will advance more slowly, and the existing U.S. advantage in technologies of relevance to defense and national security will narrow. One must be mindful of this relationship in reforming export controls for the post Cold-War period.[21]

It is difficult to quantify the full costs to U.S. companies from export controls, but the stakes are high. The global marketplace in high technology is an area where U.S. firms traditionally excel; firms at the cutting edge of high technology typically derive more than 50% of their gross revenues from exports. These include Boeing, the leading U.S. exporter, and Sun Microsystems, at the forefront in computer workstations. These firms spend large amounts in R&D for new products, at great risk, and hope to recoup their investment through export sales and increased world-wide market shares. Reductions in sales, whatever the cause, translate into reduced earnings for reinvestment in future products. This cycle, in the long term, could damage the position of U.S. firms in international markets and eventually could lessen the qualitative advantage of U.S. technologies, including those commercial technologies of relevance to national defense.

III. National Security Implications Of Export Controls On High-Performance Computing

With the disintegration of the Soviet Union, concerns about nuclear proliferation have taken center-stage in U.S. national security planning, and a successful non-proliferation strategy will require export controls on critical items. There is, however, a misunderstanding among some about the role of high technology, particularly high-performance computers (HPC), in nuclear weapons development. We next examine this issue, and consider also the role of HPC in other critical defense areas including the design and development of advanced conventional weapons and in cryptography.

High-Performance Computers and Nuclear Weapons Proliferation

Nuclear proliferation has been cited as a principal reason for controlling computers, and until just last year U.S. firms had to secure an individual validated license to ship computers with a performance of 12.5 million theoretical operations per second (Mtops) or above to destinations in certain states not party to the Non-Proliferation Treaty.[1] This is the performance level of a personal computer employing an Intel 80486 microprocessor operating at 33 MHz, a commodity product in most of the world today.

But it is a myth that powerful computers are essential in designing nuclear weapons. The United States designed its first atomic bombs in the 1940s with no electronic computers at all, using hand calculations and simple adding machines.[2] Of course, the bombs were simple, single-stage designs, were large and heavy, and, thus, were deliverable to great distance only with the use of large bombers such as the B-29. By the mid-1950s, the United States had developed relatively small-diameter nuclear artillery shells, and made the conceptual breakthrough to practical thermonuclear designs. This was done using computer power in the range of 10^{-2} Mflops, which is several orders of magnitude below the power of today's PCs. By 1970, the United States was developing small, lightweight, very sophisticated designs for strategic SLBM warheads using computer systems such as the Model 6600 from Control Data Corporation, which had a computational power in the range of 1 to 10 Mflops—the performance level of today's relatively primitive desktop PCs, which have been decontrolled for years because of their wide availability. We can reasonably conclude that today's powerful computers, although they would be of use to a proliferant, are not an "enabling" technology in nuclear weapons design and development. Less powerful, uncontrolled computers would work just fine.

Indeed, even if U.S. export controls were airtight in denying proliferant nuclear programs physical access to current workstations, this would neither prevent, nor delay for a significant period, a nuclear "wannabe" from designing and building workable nuclear weapons. States can circumvent controls in a variety of ways.[3] A country can use dedicated computers of lower performance to carry out necessary weapons calculations. It could upgrade low- and mid-range systems with accelerator boards, which are readily available and difficult to control. It could build high-performance computers indigenously, for example, by linking together arrays of microprocessors to produce parallel systems (See Appendix II). Or, it could acquire the necessary systems from sources outside the United States.[4] Most significantly, potential proliferators do not even have to import high-performance computers purchased in the United States; rather, the necessary calculations could be performed via a remote Internet connection between a foreign research institute and a computer based in the United States. In such circumstances, and with possible exceptions being the most advanced systems on the market, attempts to control computational capability may be doomed to failure.[5]

Some argue that the U.S. nuclear weapons design laboratories exploit the most advanced supercomputers in weapons development and, thus, other countries need them too. The nuclear labs do, indeed, acquire state-of-the-art supercomputers. Typically, this capability enables nuclear designers to do more of the same sorts of calculations that they had been doing previously, and has permitted the development of new warheads with fewer and fewer nuclear as well as non-nuclear tests. Some new calculations that can be carried out at the higher computational power available today permit designers to gain better understanding of the complex physical processes associated with the operation of nuclear weapons. One of the most important examples is the sophisticated three-dimensional calculations of one-point safety that are facilitated with computing power in the range of tens of thousands of Mflops.[6] The key point, however, is that emerging nuclear states will be more interested in getting a few weapons to the field, than in having scientists explore the details of weapons operation in order to shave a few pounds from the design, or implement advanced nuclear safety features. Getting a few relatively unsophisticated weapons into the field requires only modest calculational capability.[7]

Computers, however, are important, if not essential, in certain areas of warhead manufacture. Precision machine tools, some of which depend upon advanced microprocessors for numerical control, are used to manufacture key components, including rotors for uranium-enrichment centrifuges and plutonium or enriched uranium parts for nuclear weapons. But the key element of these machines is not the computer or microprocessor itself, but the control system and software that translate computer calculations into, for example, the precise movement of a lathe. Export controls on these units and their key components have not been eliminated, nor should they be.

It is much more important to focus nuclear non-proliferation controls, not on computers, but on nuclear materials, including plutonium and enriched uranium, and the means for producing them. The remarkable computer decontrol undertaken by the administration over the past two years, summarized in Table 4, was partly in recognition of this fact.

High-Performance Computers and Advanced Conventional Weapons

Nowhere has the importance of having technologically superior conventional forces been better shown than in Desert Storm. The United States and coalition forces dealt Iraq's army a devastating blow, but with losses to friendly troops that were a factor of ten lower than the lowest predictions of casualties prior to the operation. The precision air strikes carried out by coalition forces destroyed critical military installations and equipment with relatively low losses to non-combatants and relatively low collateral damage. The capability to counter military aggression decisively, and at relatively low cost, was critical to the liberation of Kuwait. It may also assist in deterring future regional aggression by instilling a new element of caution in potential aggressors. U.S. advanced defense technology created this capability and it is prudent to use export controls and other means to prevent a potential adversary from acquiring it, or from acquiring a capability to counter it.

Powerful computers have been important in creating a U.S. technological lead in its airborne reconnaissance-strike force. This force is a "system of systems," which integrates reconnaissance and intelligence assets, command and control, defense suppression, and precision strike into a very substantial military capability. The higher end of HPC is used in the design of key components of this force, such as advanced aircraft. Less powerful computers are incorporated into the platforms themselves.

U.S. Computer Controls	Regulations Before De-Control (Pre-September 1993) Mtops	Announcement of Goals (September 1993) Mtops	Regulations After De-control (Post-March 1994) Mtops
No Export License Required (IVL)	≤ 12.5	≤ 500	G-Dest: ≤ 260 Supplement 4: ≤ 500 GFW: ≤ 1000 GLX: ≤ 1000
Export License Required (IVL)	12.5 to 195	500 to 2000	≥ 260 to 1500
"Supercomputer" (License and Safeguards required)	≥ 195	≥ 2000	≥ 1500

Table 4: Trends in computer performance thresholds for triggering various export controls are indicated. Thresholds have increased an order of magnitude and more since September 1993. The "Supplement 4" license applies to states for which the U.S. has special concerns about nuclear proliferation. GFW applies to most free world countries. GLX applies to non-military activities in states of the former Warsaw Pact and China. Note that more restrictive controls (including embargoes) are in force for a few countries. The unit—Mtops (millions of theoretical operations per second)—is used by the Commerce Department to rate computer performance. For example, a 486 PC operating at 33 MHz has a performance rating of about 12.5 Mtops. A Pentium PC operating at 66 MHz has a rating of about 67 Mtops.

Very powerful computers have permitted significant advances in such areas as signature control, stealth, computational fluid dynamics, and signal and image processing. These techniques are important in the design of advanced flight vehicles. Recall the F-117A stealth aircraft, so critical to neutralizing the Iraqi integrated air defenses during the initial stage of Desert Storm without the loss of a single aircraft. The unique, multifaceted F-117A airframe, consisting of flat surfaces intersecting at seemingly random angles, was dictated by the computational capability available during its development in the late 1970s. The radar cross-section calculations were so complex and time-consuming that only a design of simple flat surfaces could be sufficiently well-calculated. No doubt, the incorporation of stealth in the F-117A compromised the aerodynamic flight characteristics of the vehicle. One has only to look at the next generation stealth fighter, the sleek F-22, to see how advances in computer technology have permitted stealth designs that are much more aerodynamically efficient.

But advances in stealth, such as those incorporated into the F-22, have relied on state-of-the-art computers with powers of tens of thousands of Mtops, well beyond the level previously characterized by the Commerce Department as "supercomputer" (195 Mtops) and even well beyond the current threshold of 1500 Mtops. Indeed, the Defense Department is actively pursuing massively parallel computer architectures in the range of millions of Mtops. Such capability is useful, among other things, in the development of "smart skins" for low radar cross-section aircraft and ships.

DoD is not only exploiting HPC in designing advanced defense platforms; it is incorporating ever-increasing computational power into the platforms themselves: in seeker and radar systems, for data fusion, image processing, automatic target recognition, and a variety of other subsystems. Because of the world-wide availability of increasingly powerful computers, however, any advantages will reside more with those who get technology into the field the fastest, and less so with those who are best at trying to prevent others from acquiring the technology.

Thus, it is at the upper reaches of computer performance where the key leverage resides for maintaining a U.S. technological lead in advanced stealth aircraft and other high-technology conventional weapons. Of course, computers are only a small part of what is needed to develop and produce a modern combat aircraft, and there are only three or four countries in the world that have a defense R&D and industrial base sufficient to exploit state-of-the-art supercomputing for developing stealth aircraft. Only a few potential enemies, including Russia and perhaps China, could exploit supercomputers to create other high-technology weapons equivalent to those of the United States.[8]

High-Performance Computers and Cryptography

Exports of high-performance computers and supercomputers are controlled because of concerns that they could be used by foreign entities to break sensitive, encoded communications of the U.S. government or its citizens.[9] Although the United States is acknowledged to have a technical lead in cryptography—the science of generating and breaking codes—one cannot foreclose the possibility that a sophisticated foreign intelligence organization could exploit powerful computers to uncover a "shortcut" weakness in a government encryption algorithm. Nor can one predict what other innovative uses of computers in cryptography could jeopardize the future security of government communications.

Even if the codes the U.S. government currently uses to protect its most sensitive communications are unbreakable in a practical sense, encrypted messages generated using weaker codes and sent by third parties (e.g., U.S. allies or domestic firms) could be intercepted and deciphered by adversaries, possibly revealing information harmful to U.S. national or economic security. Similarly, codes used in previous years to protect sensitive U.S. communications might now, assuming the messages were intercepted and stored, be susceptible to attack with modern computers. The continued secrecy of such messages may not now be vital to the country's security, but the release of such information could be politically embarrassing or otherwise undesirable.

Exports of powerful computers are also controlled in order to limit their use by foreign organizations charged with communications security. The more powerful the computer, the greater the volume of message traffic that can be encrypted in a given time. Also, supercomputers assist in the development and testing of sophisticated, highly secure encryption techniques. In either case, one result would be an increased burden on the ability of U.S. intelligence to collect and exploit foreign communications. The Intelligence Community no doubt would press for continued export controls on powerful computers in order to limit their use for such purposes. If nothing else, it is argued, continued controls are an impediment to foreign research in cryptography and thus help to maintain a U.S. lead in this critical area.

Let us consider in more detail the role of powerful computers in code breaking.

Cryptanalysis—the study of how to break codes—has existed since codes were first used. There are several different types of attacks that can be used to decipher encrypted messages and these can generally be grouped in two categories: shortcut and brute-force. In a shortcut attack, the cryptanalyst exploits the structural weaknesses of an encryption algorithm to discover either the plaintext (non-encoded) message or the key with which the message was encrypted.[10] Some encryption algorithms intentionally include a "trap door," whereby the attacker (or computer system administrator, in a less hostile scenario) can decrypt the message without using the message key. Although such loopholes are not inconceivable, today's well-tested encryption algorithms are thought not to have such weaknesses. This forces cryptanalysts to rely on the second method of attack: brute-force.

Brute-force, or exhaustive search attacks require that the adversary attempt all possible keys until one is found that will decrypt the message. This requires a powerful computing system to generate keys rapidly and apply them to the coded communications. The key-length determines how many keys are possible, and hence the calculational resources required to decipher encrypted messages into meaningful plaintext. Specifically, a key-length of X bits has 2^X possible keys. For example, the Data Encryption Standard (DES) algorithm (the U.S. government standard for unclassified communications) uses 56-bit keys; there are thus 2^{56} (approximately 10^{17}) possible keys. On average, half the keys (or 2^{55} keys) would be tried before the right key was found.

In 1977, Diffie and Hellman examined the characteristics of a hybrid computer that could carry out a brute-force, known-plaintext attack on a DES-encrypted message.[11] Given a system consisting of 10^6 special DES encryption chips operating in parallel, with each chip able to test 10^6 keys per second, a search of 10^{17} keys could be conducted in about one day (10^5 seconds). The order-of-magnitude cost of such a system was estimated to be about $20 million (1977 dollars). More recently, Michael Weiner claims that with mature technology one could build a machine for about $1 million (1993 dollars) to carry out an exhaustive DES key search in an average time of 3.5 hours. This machine would use 60,000 processors operating in parallel; each processor would be a fully pipelined DES search chip operating at 50 MHz and capable of testing about 50 million keys per second.[12] Such approaches may be feasible for sophisticated national or sub-national groups, and if so are certainly affordable.

It is noteworthy that these hybrid systems are not the typical supercomputer sold by Cray or Hitachi. Rather, they are specialized systems with hardware optimized to carry out efficient key searches in connection with a specific encryption algorithm. It would be possible, of course, to do key searches in software using commercial supercomputers, but it would be considerably slower. For example, a software implementation of the classified SKIPJACK algorithm optimized for a single processor on the eight-processor Cray YMP supercomputer would perform about 10^5 key searches per second. Using all eight processors and "aggressive vectorization" would increase the capacity of the system by two to three orders of magnitude, still much below the capacity of the specialized machines described above.[13]

A brute force attack can be made impractical by increasing the number of bits in the key. For example, assuming the cost of processing power is halved every eighteen months, it would take 36 years before SKIPJACK (80-bit key) would be as vulnerable as DES (56-bit key) is today. Alternatively, assuming a hypothetical attack using a parallel configuration of 1.2 billion SKIPJACK processors, each costing $1 and operating at a clock speed of 1 GHz, it would take one year to exhaust the SKIPJACK key space.[14]

Thus, we see that the specialized, massively parallel, hybrid computing systems described above are the most relevant for code breaking, assuming a manageable key space. Attempts to restrain foreign capabilities in this area would seem to center around controlling the special chips peculiar to specific encryption algorithms used to code and decode messages. Commercial supercomputers seem less useful in brute-force code breaking, but could be important in other cryptographic applications, such as the generation of secure codes or the search for "trap doors" in an adversary's codes. Continued controls on these systems are warranted at levels consonant with maintaining the U.S. lead in this critical area. Specifically, controls could be maintained at computer performance levels in the range of one to two orders-of-magnitude below the performance of the computers currently in use by the U.S. government for cryptographic applications.

Conclusions and Recommendations

Export controls on high-performance computers are of little relevance in restraining nuclear weapons proliferation. Rather, the high-end supercomputers are where the key leverage resides for the United States in keeping its technological lead in such areas as advanced conventional weapons and cryptography. Moreover, computers at the highest performance levels are more controllable because there are currently only two supplier countries—the United States and Japan—and they often agree on the undesirable endusers.[15] Alternatively, there is little value in trying to control computers at performance levels below a few thousand Mtops; these systems are much less useful in advanced conventional weapons design or in cryptography. This argument applies to other key defense capabilities including detection of submarines using large ASW arrays.

Export controls should, therefore, focus on maintaining the U.S. technological lead in "true" supercomputers without affecting sales of less powerful systems. The recent U.S. decision to raise the supercomputer control threshold a factor of ten above the previous threshold was consistent with this principle. In summary, we find that:

- *Controls on computers at the 10-1000 Mtops range or above are unlikely to impede emerging nuclear weapons programs.* Our analysis thus supports the recent relaxation of lower-end computer controls.

- *Some controls on supercomputers, those having performance levels at the current state of the art (10,000-100,000 Mtops and above), will continue to be in the U.S. interest.* It is the "true" supercomputers that provide the greatest leverage in maintaining our lead in advanced defense technology. Export control thresholds could be set one or two orders of magnitude below the state-of-the-art systems currently in use by the U.S. defense industry and the Intelligence Community.

- *Continue export controls on specialized encryption chips and related hardware as mandated under the ITARs.* Pay particularly close attention to export license requests for large shipments of these devices.

- *In implementing controls in general, consider not only the technology itself but the degree to which specific states can exploit it to develop WMD or threaten the U.S. lead in advanced conventional arms or in code breaking.* There are only a few states in the world considered potentially hostile to the United States who are able to exploit high technology to create, for example, an indigenous reconnaissance-strike force, or a capability to counter one. For those who are unable, the best approach is not so much to worry about their acquisition of high technology, but to convince suppliers of advanced weapons systems not to sell to them.

IV. Export Controls On Microprocessors

In this section, we examine the question of export controls on microprocessors.[1] We examine the controllability of these devices and their foreign availability, including that resulting from their manufacture overseas. We review trends in the export control of microprocessors, and assess why controls on these devices have been relatively less stringent than they have been for other high-technology products including computers. Based on controllability arguments, we conclude that export controls on microprocessors themselves should be lifted, but that greater caution be exercised in the dissemination of the associated production technology.

As discussed earlier, it is difficult to quantify the economic costs of export controls, and the case for microprocessors is no different. We do, however, examine qualitatively one important economic impact: how have past export controls on microprocessors affected the computer industry, the chief consumer of these devices. Using advanced microprocessors as an example, we illustrate how, in today's global economy, U.S. high-technology export controls have been rendered ineffective while creating advantages for foreign competitors in overseas markets.

Background

The microprocessor is the primary hardware component of modern computers and has enabled the revolution in information technology.[2] Beyond computing, the microprocessor has critical defense applications in such areas as sophisticated telecommunications, data security, avionics, and guided weapons systems. Driven by the personal computer industry, microprocessors sales constitute the fastest growing sector of the semiconductor industry, doubling in size every four to five years.[3]

Overall, global semiconductor sales were more than $77 billion in 1993 with U.S. firms grossing $33 billion or 43% of the market; by 1996, that figure is expected to reach $100 billion.[4] Semiconductor export revenues to U.S. firms reached $20 billion in 1993.

Merchant semiconductor manufacturing (where firms produce for the open market) is one of the world's fastest growing industrial sectors; U.S.

firms have a near monopoly on the high end of this market: the advanced microprocessor. Indeed, most advanced microprocessors are either of U.S. origin or are manufactured abroad using licensed U.S. technology.[5] The top seven manufacturers in 1993 were all U.S. producers. Between them they split 93% of the global microprocessor market, earning revenues of $8.3 billion from a total for all firms of $8.9 billion.[6] The industry shipped more than 45 million advanced units in 1993 with shipments of more than 100 million expected by 1997.[7]

Controllability, Foreign Availability and Licensed Production Abroad

Since microprocessors are no more than a few square centimeters in size, they are easy to conceal and difficult to control. One suitcase can carry many hundreds, worth hundreds of thousands of dollars. Large quantities can be legally purchased in one country and then smuggled to another; it is not easy for customs officials or law enforcement to curtail such shipments. For instance, Iran has obtained advanced Intel microprocessors on the black market, even though the product is not authorized for export or re-export to that country.[8]

Theft or illegal diversion from production factories and warehouses is also a common method for acquiring these devices. There have been a number of such incidents over the years.[9] In 1979, ten thousand chips were stolen from an Intel production line in 1979. Another Silicon Valley firm, Monolithic Memories, lost 20% of a several-million dollar inventory from a single theft in 1981.[10] Recent press reports suggest that microprocessors have become some of the most valued commodities on international black markets.[11] Theft and diversion, however, are unreliable as a means of acquiring a stable product supply, manufacturer support, or custom-designed chips; nor are they a likely approach to acquiring substantial microprocessor production technology.

Even without theft or diversion, advanced microprocessors are becoming more widely available on foreign markets. In recent years, U.S. semiconductor and microprocessor companies have built fabrication facilities overseas, or have licensed their production technology to foreign producers in Europe and Asia. Besides those in Japan, companies in South Korea, Taiwan, and Singapore have emerged recently as significant suppliers. South Korea's Samsung, Germany's Siemens, the Dutch firm Philips, and other foreign firms listed in Table 5 are all licensed by U.S. companies to manufacture and export advanced microprocessors.

U.S. chip manufacturers have increasingly moved their production offshore for strong economic reasons: to lower costs and to gain better access

U.S. COMPANY	FOREIGN LICENSEES
DEC	Olivetti
Hewlett-Packard	Hitachi, Mitsubishi, Oki, Samsung, Winbond
SGI-MIPS	NEC, Siemens, Sony, Toshiba, Macronix
Sun Microsystems	Fujitsu, Matsushita, Philips, Toshiba

Table 5: Selected Major 32-Bit RISC Microprocessors Under Licensed Foreign Production (1993-1994). [Source: William J. McClean, ed., *Status 1993: A Report of the Integrated Circuit Industry* (Integrated Circuit Engineering Corporation, 1993), p. 6-34; and multiple press reports.]

COUNTRY	DOMESTIC COMPANY
France	SGS Thompson (through Cyrix)
Japan	NEC, VM Technologies
Korea	Samsung, Hyundai (?)
Taiwan	United Microelectronics
United States	AMD, Cyrix, Chips & Technologies, DEC (in Scotland), IBM, Texas Instruments (cross licensed through Cyrix, Chips & Technologies)

Table 6: Producers of Advanced Intel-Type 32-Bit Microprocessors (1993) [Source: William J. McClean, ed., *Status 1993: A Report of the Integrated Circuit Industry* (Integrated Circuit Engineering Corporation, 1993), p. 6-34; and multiple press reports.]

to regional markets such as the Far East, the industry's fastest growing market. Market access was also a key factor in Intel's siting of fabrication plants in Ireland and Israel, and in the company's growing interest in China. In March 1994, Intel entered a first-of-its-kind partnership with China's major state-run electronics firm, China Electronics Corporation, to market Intel microprocessors in China. In return, Intel agreed to let a contract with a subsidiary of China Electronics to test and assemble Intel 386 chips. Experience gained in such a relationship could forge the groundwork for the eventual production of Intel chips in China.[12]

Other developers of high-end microprocessors, such as Sun Microsystems and Hewlett-Packard, have licensed their technology to numerous overseas competitors in order to expand the potential market for the computers on which they are based, and to establish their microprocessor architectures as industry standards. These practices have helped accelerate the global transfer of information and know-how for producing advanced microelectronics.[13]

There are a few foreign firms that produce advanced microprocessors using their own design and production technology and that compete with U.S. manufacturers.[14] Although Japan is the United States' chief competitor, in 1992 other foreign producers captured 6% of the multi-billion dollar global market in microprocessors.[15] There are at least five world-class fabrication plants on-line in Taiwan, with others on the way. Government support and ongoing factory expansion efforts should result soon in Taiwanese firms acquiring a capability to produce state-of-the-art memory devices; and at least one Taiwan firm has designed and manufactured microprocessors that substitute for Intel's 486 chip.[16] Other firms with similar capabilities are noted in Table 6. Struggling companies like Germany's Siemens continue to remain in the market, producing mainly for Europe. Along with Taiwan, other states, such as South Korea and Israel, have made it national policy to promote the domestic growth of advanced semiconductor manufacturing.

As we might expect, the wide foreign availability of advanced microprocessors coupled with their small physical size and volume sales has fundamentally undermined the potential for effective export control of these devices.[17]

Trends in Microprocessor Export Controls

As with computers, the export of microprocessors has been controlled under authority of the Export Administration Act (EAA).[18] The specific rules governing these devices are complex and have been amended numerous times over the years. Starting in the mid-1980s, successive legislative and regulatory actions initiated a process of decontrol that has contributed to the wide foreign availability of U.S. microprocessors. Purely commercial items having embedded microprocessors, including toys and medical equipment, were exempted from mandatory licensing requirements in 1985.

When Congress amended the EAA in 1988, it also included provisions to exempt any foreign-made product from U.S. re-export controls if the total value of U.S.-controlled components in that product was less than 25% of the product's value.[19] This freed up from U.S. re-export controls many foreign products that employed advanced U.S. microprocessors. In 1990, the United States authorized exporters of semiconductors to ship to most non-Communist destinations without having to seek prior government approval.

Today, microprocessor exports are virtually unrestricted, except to Russia and China, and to states involved in international terrorist activities such as Iran and Syria. For these states, exports of microprocessors with technical specifications that exceed an Intel 386/40MHz chip still require a license, even though personal computers based on chips comparable to the 386 are no longer marketable, at least in the United States.

Thus, microprocessor producers have escaped U.S. export controls relatively unscathed. Indeed, one of industry's biggest concerns is to avoid a rollback of recent legislative and regulatory liberalization.[20] A limited rollback on the most advanced microprocessors, however, might not cut into the profits of U.S. suppliers because, in the current competitive environment, they would probably continue to dominate the market.[21] A more substantial rollback, such as one that imposes controls on lower performance chips, would be more damaging. In the one area where significant controls remain (shipments to certain of the former CoCom-target states), it has not been costly to U.S. producers because the commercial market for semiconductors in the former Eastern Bloc has been small relative to the non-Communist world. This may change as China and the East European states modernize their economies and infrastructure.[22]

The dissemination of microprocessor technology by U.S. corporations has greatly complicated the task of export controls. It is now much more difficult to ensure that U.S.-origin microprocessors, or those manufactured abroad with U.S. technology, will be controlled by host governments.[23] Even if foreign governments do control exports of domestic products that incorporate U.S.-controlled technology or components, they typically do not seek rights to control any further re-exports. Such products can be produced abroad and receive U.S. permission for export to a third country, but even if that country does impose its own export controls, potential adversaries can still acquire the product. For instance, Sun Microsystems' powerful SPARC microprocessors are manufactured in Japan under license to Matsushita and Fujitsu. The United States would likely approve the export of these items from Japan to Taiwan for assembly in workstations. However, there is little to stop the Taiwan firm from exporting those workstations to whomever it wants, including destinations to which similar U.S. products are controlled.[24]

Recently, export controls have had a negative impact on U.S. firms in a new area. With the end of the Cold War, U.S. firms are moving to engage scientists and engineers in the former Soviet bloc in joint ventures involving high technology. Some firms are finding this a productive, low-cost approach to generating new ideas and products. For example, Sun Microsystems has a joint venture in cooperative R&D with a Russian affiliate—the Moscow Center for SPARC Technology—to stimulate advances in microelectronics design. But Sun has had great difficulty transferring the necessary technical data to its partner because of concerns by the U.S. government that sensitive information will be compromised. Partly as a result, Sun has not received as much benefit from this venture as it had anticipated. This case is described in more detail in Appendix III. There are several other cases in which this has occurred. Technology transfer problems will become more important as high-tech firms seek greater cooperation with enterprises in the FSU and China.

Effect of Relaxed Microprocessor Export Controls on the Computer Industry

Ironically, the relaxation of microprocessor export controls has, in certain cases, actually harmed the U.S. computer industry, particularly in the personal computer and workstation market sectors. In recent years, the decontrol of advanced microprocessors has outpaced the decontrol of the computer platforms based on these microprocessors.[25] As a result, some computer makers, primarily in newly industrialized states, have been able to use U.S. microprocessors in the design and manufacture of computer clones that they then market in competition with platforms of equivalent performance sold by U.S. firms. Until very recently, however, the competition was not on a "level playing field." For example, foreign-made clones were often exported to countries, including former CoCom targets, where U.S. computers of comparable performance were denied entry. Foreign firms also gained advantage by being able to sell immediately to destinations where U.S. firms experienced significant delays due the export license application and approval process. In both cases U.S. firms were placed at a competitive disadvantage because of the disparity between microprocessor and computer controls.

As an example, Taiwan is one of the largest producers of PC clones. Its firms are largely unhampered by export controls, and tend to be only 120 days behind U.S. manufacturers in introducing comparable product lines. Export licensing delays can thus reduce "first to market" advantages for U.S. producers. In this connection, Table 7 shows that potential "competitiveness gaps" of up to three years have occurred from the time computers manufactured in Taiwan were openly available on international markets, to the time when U.S. computers of comparable performance became fully decontrolled.

The recent relaxation of computer controls summarized in Table 4 has eased the problem for the time being. But the pace of technological progress is so rapid that microprocessors now in development will, as soon as they are released, exceed, or come close to exceeding, today's performance thresholds for computer export controls.[26] When this occurs U.S. exporters will be at a competitive disadvantage until thresholds are raised once again. A balance can be struck by routinely raising the control threshold on computer performance as each new generation of microprocessors is introduced, making controls more responsive to the pace of technology. This process is called "indexing." Legislation introduced in 1993 would have established an indexing system to adjust performance thresholds upward as technologies advance.[27]

Alternatively, some argue that microprocessors should be controlled at the performance level of their associated computer platforms. This approach is unlikely to be workable for a number of reasons. First, as we have pointed out, there is the inherent difficulty in controlling transfers of these small components—several hundred of which could fit in a suitcase. Second, controlling microprocessors is unlikely, in the long run, to restrain overall computing power, given that high-performance parallel processors can be developed by linking together arrays of microprocessors, each with a performance level below the control threshold. (Appendix II offers more details about the implications of the microprocessor for high-performance, massively parallel computing.) Export controls on microprocessors, if extensively rolled back, could cause foreign firms with the requisite technology to develop and produce new microprocessor architectures at or above restricted performance levels. As a result, such a policy could create competitors in an area where U.S. firms currently have a near monopoly. Finally, controls are impractical because microprocessor production technology has already been disseminated widely by U.S. firms who have licensed production rights to their designs to manufacturers in Europe and Asia.

U.S. Origin Microprocessor	Year Taiwanese Computers Introduced	Year Controls Lifted on U.S. Computers*	U.S.-Taiwan Competitiveness Gap (Approx.)**
Intel 286	1988†	Aug 1989	1 year
Intel 386	1988	Jul 1990	2 years
Intel 486	1989	Sep 1991	2 years
Cypress SPARC	1990	Jan 1994	3 years
Intel 486DX	1990	Jan 1994	3 years
Intel 486DX(multi)	1992††	Jan 1994	2 years
Pentium	1993††	Jan 1994	6-8 months

* Date beyond which no U.S. license is required to export equivalent computers to any destination, except those still controlled for foreign policy reasons (e.g., Iran or Iraq).

** Potential competitiveness gap between U.S. and Taiwanese computer makers created by CoCom-based export controls. During the period of the "gap", a U.S. company would have had, at minimum, to apply for an export license for sales to proscribed states, while a non-CoCom/5(k) country, such as Taiwan, would not. In some cases added U.S. non-proliferation controls may also have restricted or delayed U.S. access to markets in some countries to the advantage of all foreign competitors.

† A Taiwan computer based on the 286 was introduced in 1984. At that time, exports of computers based on the 286 were subject to U.S. export and re-export controls which treated domestic and foreign firms comparably. In 1988, however, a change in U.S. re-export controls (the "de minimus exemption") resulted in the effective decontrol to the Soviet bloc of 286 computers produced in states not members of CoCom.

†† Year Commerce Department officially finds computers at this level available to proscribed destinations.

Table 7: Potential U.S.-Taiwan Competitiveness Gap in Computers

Recommendations

- *Indexing should be adopted to allow for timely, coordinated decontrol of microprocessors and computers prior to their becoming available from foreign sources that do not implement appropriate export controls.* An expert advisory panel could facilitate oversight. In no case should the United States continue to control a computer for which the associated microprocessor is generally available. The concern is that such microprocessors can be incorporated in foreign-made clones that (1) are exported without control, or (2) do not require U.S. re-export authorization because the value of the microprocessor does not exceed the de minimus threshold. Such a situation is highly disadvantageous to U.S. companies. Special microprocessors developed for military applications, including radiation-hardened versions, would remain subject to controls.

- *Export controls should be fully lifted on microprocessors now under general commercial distribution or where the production technology is widely licensed abroad.* Sun's current SPARC line, Intel's x86 series (including the Pentium), and the newly released PowerPC chips exemplify processors requiring export licenses to certain destinations. Because there is no effective way to monitor or control microprocessor exports, continued regulation imposes an anti-competitive burden on U.S. exporters. A limited category of the most advanced U.S. microprocessors could continue to be controlled, but only if U.S. firms remain sole source suppliers and product quantities remain limited. High-end chips produced for the multiprocessor workstation market might fit this category.

- *The U.S. government should take a fresh look at the national security and economic costs and benefits of transferring abroad potentially sensitive technology and know-how for the manufacture of dual-use, high-technology products, including microprocessors.* Items manufactured abroad with U.S.-licensed technology cannot be controlled as effectively as in the United States. Furthermore, the dissemination of such knowledge naturally strengthens indigenous capabilities for manufacture. The choice between denying exports of manufacturing technologies (at the expense of the commercial interests of U.S. firms), and promulgating them under conditions that make controls infeasible, requires a thoughtful cost-benefit analysis in each case.

- *Antiquated controls on transfers of technical or proprietary data should be relaxed in the case of U.S. firms trying to engage in cooperative R&D ventures with commercial partners in the former Soviet bloc.* Caution must still be exercised because of the potential that such information could be used in military programs, but we expect that the potential downside in this regard would be small for many of the ventures involving collaboration in basic research. In many cases, the transfer of data of real significance produced in the venture is one-way into the United States.

V. Export Controls On Mass-Market Software With Encryption

The issue of export controls on encryption software products, including mass-market software with encryption capability, has come under recent review.[1] The U.S. government strictly controls exports of such products; its basic concern is that potential adversaries, aggressors, criminals, or criminal organizations could take advantage of difficult-to-break codes to communicate over global networks free from eavesdropping.[2] The software industry has sought to relax controls on encryption products arguing that the basic encryption algorithms are already in the public domain and it thus makes little sense to control products that utilize these same algorithms.[3]

Software with encryption capability is not treated as a dual-use item under Commerce Department export jurisdiction. Rather, exports of these items must be licensed by the State Department's Office of Defense Trade Controls, which considers encryption systems as "munitions." The State Department routinely prohibits export of all but the least sophisticated encryption packages—the exceptions being exports to foreign offices or subsidiaries of U.S. companies, or foreign financial institutions. Domestic software producers that include encryption as a feature in their retail packages often must weaken or remove entirely these portions of software in order to secure an export license.[4]

In July 1991, after heavy lobbying by the software industry, then National Security Adviser Brent Scowcroft sent a letter to Sen. Jake Garn (R-Utah)—who had pressed strongly for export control relaxation on behalf of his state's software manufacturers—announcing that licensing decisions on new software products incorporating two relatively weak encryption algorithms would be routinely transferred, after seven days, from State to Commerce for automatic approval.[5] Since 1991, no further encryption products have been added to the automatic-approval list although Scowcroft, in a follow-up statement, noted that the government had agreed to an industry request for semiannual meetings to review newer schemes for further decontrol.

Legislation to decontrol encryption products utilizing a variety of popular schemes was introduced by Rep. Maria Cantwell (D-Washington) in November 1993.[6] Similar legislation was introduced in the Senate. There were three key provisions:

- It transfers from State to Commerce jurisdiction over exports of information security technology, including encryption software, except for products specifically designed for military use.

- No validated license may be required for the export of mass market or public-domain software with encryption capabilities, except for exports to countries proscribed by the Trading with the Enemy Act.

- Commerce must grant licenses to export encryption software to countries for which the export of such software is already approved for use by financial institutions, unless such software is likely to be directed to military or terrorist end-use.

Elements of the government have opposed the transfer of jurisdiction over encryption exports from State to Commerce citing several reasons.[7] There is concern that NSA's ability to monitor new commercial products and technologies in connection with its review of export licenses would be weakened. Some fear that Commerce's controls are inadequate when compared with those that State exercises over munitions. In the past, the transfer of jurisdiction of an item from State to Commerce has often led to its eventual decontrol. Within State, approved licenses for foreign military sales, including those for preexisting contracts, can be revoked or suspended; Commerce does not have this right in regard to dual-use exports unless the President certifies an overriding need to Congress. State controls items on a global basis whereas Commerce's controls generally apply only to specific destinations. As a result, items on the dual-use list could be transferred to proscribed states by re-export through a third party.[8] Finally, munitions items are not subject to determinations of foreign availability as is generally the case for items on the dual-use list. A principal disadvantage in keeping jurisdiction with State is that Commerce has no rights to review munitions licensing decisions made by State; thus the commercial interests of U.S. firms must be factored in through other channels. On the other hand, items on the dual-use list are reviewed by State and Defense in connection with U.S. national security and foreign policy interests.

In June 1994, the House Foreign Affairs Committee reported its version of the Export Administration Act of 1994 (EAA), which included the Cantwell provisions. In subsequent deliberations, the House Select Committee on Intelligence removed them. The bill, however, was marked "open" by the House Rules Committee, which permitted Cantwell to offer an amendment prior to floor debate, essentially restoring her original provisions. The prospect of an acrimonious floor debate prompted Vice President Gore to write to Cantwell offering certain concessions, including U.S. government agreement to examine alternatives to the use of key escrow encryption in computer networks.[9] In return, Cantwell agreed not to offer her amendment.

The Gore-Cantwell "compromise"—if it can be called that—foreclosed the prospect for substantive decontrol of encryption products until a new EAA is passed and two studies analyzing these issues are completed. In one study, requested in the pending EAA, the administration is to review the current and future international market for encryption products, the impact of export controls on the competitive position of U.S. software manufacturers, and the extent that encryption software products are available from foreign producers.[10] In the other, commissioned in the 1994 Defense authorization bill, the National Research Council is to conduct an independent study of cryptographic technologies and national cryptography policy, and of the related implications for economic competitiveness, national security, law enforcement interests, and the privacy of U.S. citizens. This latter study is scheduled for completion in 1996.[11]

National Security Implications of Decontrol

U.S. national intelligence collection systems are deployed world-wide to monitor international communications signals, including voice transmissions and message traffic, to acquire communications intelligence (COMINT). Some signals are scrambled and need to be decrypted before the content of a message or conversation can be understood; many are broadcast "in the clear." NSA Director Adm. John M. McConnell has argued that information acquired from these sources is vital to the security of the United States and that "the success of NSA's intelligence mission depends on our continued ability to collect and understand foreign communications."[12]

NSA's precise concerns regarding the national security threat posed by the export of strong encryption products are classified. However, in testimony before Congress in March 1994 concerning digital telephony and its impact on court-authorized wiretaps, FBI Director Louis Freeh provided specific information about the harm to national security and domestic law enforcement if the government lost its ability to intercept and read communications. He stated:

> The nation's telecommunications networks are routinely used in the commission of serious criminal activities, including terrorism and espionage. Organized crime groups and drug trafficking organizations, which are often highly structured, rely heavily upon telecommunications to plan and execute their criminal activities and hide their illegal proceeds. Similarly, foreign intelligence service officers and their agents carry out their spy and other clandestine missions through these networks.[13]

In his testimony, Freeh cited several cases where drug smuggling, organized criminal activities, corruption, and violent crime have been thwarted or criminals brought to justice (both in the United States and abroad) by the use of electronic surveillance. Such techniques are also critical to FBI efforts to help prevent terrorism; Freeh cited instances of planned attacks against commercial airliners, a nuclear power facility, embassies and consulates, and U.S. allies overseas that were all prevented through the use of electronic surveillance.[14] Presumably, NSA's concerns, and the types of examples that it might cite, are of a similar nature.

The NSA is alarmed that the widespread use of encryption will generate a rapid increase in the volume of coded messages sent over global networks and, as a result, severely tax its ability to acquire and exploit telecommunications.[15] It is not that NSA will be less able to decipher specific coded messages; rather, the concern is that a flood of new encrypted traffic will make its job much more difficult by creating a larger "haystack" from which it must extract the "needles." Indeed, NSA can now target possible threats simply by their use of encryption and the associated premise that, because its use is still relatively limited, those who encrypt their messages may have something nefarious to hide. Simply put, if everyone encrypts, the winnowing process becomes unmanageable.[16]

The foreign availability of strong encryption algorithms cited by industry is not a big problem for NSA because the use of these algorithms in international telecommunications still remains quite limited. The reason for this is that none of the mass-market software available on foreign markets embeds encryption seamlessly into the widely used networking and workgroup software sold mainly by U.S. companies. Protecting information is an extra (and often tedious) step using the "stand-alone" (packages that encrypt information but perform no other application) encryption products generally available overseas, and thus it is simply not a widespread practice.[17]

This situation could change if U.S. software suppliers, which currently control a 75% share of the world market, were allowed to export versions of their products that employ strong encryption systems operating in background, *without user interaction.* For example, Lotus Notes, a widely used communication and cooperative-work package, has an installed base of more than 500,000 users. Every piece of electronic mail sent and every document transferred between computers using this software is automatically encrypted with a public-key scheme without the user's knowledge or input.[18] Similarly, Novell NetWare 4.0, the latest version of the country's most popular networking software, encrypts network traffic with an RSA-licensed, public-key encryption system that is transparent to the user.[19] Apple Computer's forthcoming AppleTalk Secure Data Stream Protocol and the currently available Apple Open Collaboration Environment, do the same for the approximately 10% of America's computers that can run the AppleTalk network protocol.[20]

These "hands off" encryption products are of particular concern to NSA. Their widespread use in routine telecommunications would increase significantly the volume of encrypted traffic entering and leaving the United States, as well as that transmitted between third parties overseas. Unless new ways of doing business can be found, a significant part of the U.S. investment in national COMINT collection systems could be rendered obsolete, and NSA's ability to provide key intelligence to U.S. policymakers would be impaired.

In the past NSA has adapted its methods of COMINT exploitation to accommodate major advances in communications technology. The widespread use of encryption, which seems inevitable, will no doubt bring about further changes, but the net effect on national security may not be as great as some argue. Although the use of modern communications technologies such as seamless encryption, common channel signaling, digital switches, and fiberoptic links is an impediment to intelligence collection, the NSA will still be able to collect much of the information it needs.[21] The problem will be in reading or exploiting it in some other way. In this latter regard, several important techniques are effective whether or not communications are encoded: emitter identification, in which subtle features of an emitter's radio frequency transmissions are used to identify uniquely the sender; traffic analysis, in which sender and recipient addresses and the volume, length, and time of messages (rather than their content) are analyzed; and clandestine COMINT, in which communications traffic is intercepted before it is encrypted.

Indeed, modern telecommunications technology may be as much a boon to intelligence collection as it is a complicating factor.[22] As telecommunications networks grow and business and governments become more reliant upon them, NSA may find more and better information being routed over links it can currently exploit. For example, in the past, foreign agents communicated via hidden mail drops or in face-to-face meetings at locations free from surveillance—approaches that posed obvious difficulties for intelligence and law enforcement. Now, communication is more likely to occur via secure electronic mail or telephone. Although the information may be scrambled, these channels are much more accessible to intelligence collection, and methods such as traffic analysis can assist in targeting specific, high-value channels for decryption. Over the long term, however, it remains to be seen whether new and innovative technologies for intelligence collection and exploitation will enable NSA to stay ahead of current trends towards greater use of encryption as a means of information security.

Concerns of U.S. Software Suppliers, Computer Firms, and the Business Community

While U.S. software companies may recognize the need for law enforcement and intelligence agencies to be able to gather timely and accurate information, they also see an untapped market which could generate substantial revenue. Indeed, U.S.-produced, mass-market software products (some with weak encryption as part of the package) attract overseas buyers principally as a result of the high quality and versatility of their principal application, whether it be for word processing, spreadsheet, or network application. If strong encryption were embedded in these products, it would make them even more attractive to foreign business.

According to the Software Publishers Association (SPA), domestic software suppliers' overseas sales account for approximately 40% of total revenue. The amount of increased sales that would ensue if U.S. products offered strong encryption is difficult to quantify. Complicating such calculations, among other things, is the fact that company officials are often unwilling to comment on lost business opportunities. As a result, there are no hard estimates of the "lost sales" associated with current export controls.[23] The SPA believes, however, that foreign companies in Germany, Japan, and elsewhere have recognized this market's potential and are moving to introduce niche products that will eventually decrease U.S. market share. This view is not universally held: one industry executive argues that there are no foreign software companies equivalent to a Microsoft or Novell waiting in Germany, Japan, or South Korea to take over the market if U.S. firms are unable to bundle business software with seamless, strong encryption.[24]

"Stand-alone" encryption products are available from both U.S. and foreign suppliers. These packages are designed to link with U.S. mass-market business software and require user interaction, which limits their widespread use. Because these products are already available overseas, it is not clear whether U.S. firms would reap much benefit if export controls were relaxed.[25]

There are other direct costs of export controls for encryption products. For example, U.S. suppliers often must produce two separate versions of their software, with the foreign version having weaker encryption or none at all. Producing two sets of manuals and floppy disks increases a firm's costs. Maintaining personnel familiar with export policies who deal with the government on this issue also cuts into the manufacturers' profits, and is particularly hard on small companies.[26]

Because most companies desire confidentiality in their business operations, computer systems that do not include encryption software or equivalent data security features, are not viable for many commercial applications. Officials from one computer hardware manufacturer argued that their firm cannot bid effectively for some foreign orders if it cannot include network encryption software in the overall package.[27] Are such orders then being filled by foreign firms? If they are, we might expect a substantial increase in encrypted telecommunications. But we do not know if this is the case. Even if licenses are eventually granted, however, the typical delays (often months) harm a firm's competitiveness in some markets. For this reason, U.S. hardware giants probably lose some number of important sales to overseas competitors.

The greatest impact of export controls for U.S. companies, one which is intangible and hard to quantify, may be upon their business operations. There is a potential for great increases in efficiency and reduced costs if companies can link closely with customers and suppliers over modern global telecommunications networks. For example, companies that currently use overnight shippers for sensitive documents would have much more flexibility if this information could be transmitted electronically. But firms must be assured that proprietary information including customer base, sales negotiations, and trade secrets are protected (especially from foreign intelligence surveillance), and thus they will require access to strong encryption for many business communications.[28] To the degree that export controls discourage the use of modern telecommunications in their global operations, firms will not reap the benefits of increased productivity and may become less competitive in the long term. This is not to mention the value of proprietary data lost when a firm uses these networks but lacks effective communications security. Indeed, the cost to U.S. firms from industrial espionage has been estimated by some to be in the range of billions of dollars per year, and this could grow if corporations must rely more on insecure telecommunications systems.[29]

Foreign Controls on the Export (and Use) of Encryption Products

The United States is not alone among governments interested in regulating the dissemination and widespread use of data encryption products. France not only imposes strict export controls, but it also controls imports and domestic use of these products. It requires citizens to register and use government-approved encryption systems. Violations of France's cryptographic laws can result in from one to three months imprisonment, fines running from six to fifty thousand Francs, confiscation of cryptographic equipment or software, and denial for a period of two years of the right to apply for permission to use cryptographic products.[30]

In the United Kingdom, cryptographic products are controlled similarly to the United States. Britain has followed CoCom guidelines governing the export of encryption products and technologies.[31] It does not impose import or domestic use controls. Exports of items using the A5 encryption algorithm, such as in the GSM digital cellular phones and related network hardware and software, are routinely denied to countries not part of CoCom (or its follow-on regime) nor part of the Conference of European Postal and Telecommunications administrations (CEPT).[32] Britain, concerned about the dissemination of encryption systems world-wide, has initiated discussions with the European Standards Institute to develop a weaker algorithm than A5 for export to these states. France has also reportedly opposed exports of systems using A5.

While countries such as Denmark have no rules governing the domestic use of encryption products, other European states have recently begun to consider the need. During 1994, legislation similar to current French law was introduced in Holland and Germany to control public access to encryption systems.[33] Press reports indicate that there have been discussions within some governments in Europe about the possibility of adopting a European standard for key escrow cryptography along the lines of Clipper.[34] Taiwan, South Korea, and China prohibit the private use of encryption.[35]

Thus, even if U.S. firms were permitted to export encryption products at will, the import controls that some governments currently impose may restrain the market to a degree. In addition, other states could have increased incentive to impose similar controls on imports.

Conclusions and Recommendations

In trying to address substantively the data security and encryption issue, it is clear that there are many uncertainties. We have the fundamental problem of trying to gauge national security interests without access to classified information, and the related problem that good data does not exist for assessing the economic impact of export controls and the impact on a company from not practicing good communications security in domestic and overseas operations. Let us summarize what we do know, and from there see what recommendations might be sensible.

First, strong encryption algorithms and associated software are in the public domain, but these technologies have not been put to widespread use globally. As a result, they seem to have not yet created insurmountable problems for U.S. intelligence. The NSA is concerned, however, that this will change if U.S.-produced mass-market software with embedded strong encryption becomes widely available overseas. It would result in an explosive increase in encrypted message traffic, and software industry groups, including the SPA, do not dispute this. Such an outcome will complicate NSA's job by decreasing its ability to perform broad keyword searches and taxing the capacity of computers used in decoding. There appears to be a strong case that this would harm national security.

Second, the shift towards encryption is an inevitable outgrowth of the technological revolution in telecommunications. The rapid flow of information is itself of tangible value. For this reason alone, there exists a clear need to protect and authenticate communications. Moreover, U.S. firms must be prepared to compete globally. This means that they must develop efficient ways to communicate with customers and suppliers throughout the world. If U.S. firms are unable to assure the privacy of communications with these entities, they become increasingly vulnerable to industrial espionage.

Thus, national security arguments do not necessarily override the software industry's case. Indeed, economic security is becoming more and more a part of national security. U.S. firms and their overseas subsidiaries, partners, customers, and competitors rely a great deal on modern telecommunications and this reliance is likely to grow in the future. Because information security will be important for engaging these markets, and because the global and widespread use of encryption seems inevitable, the longer such use is blocked by concerns over intelligence-gathering complications, the greater the potential harm to U.S. economic interests.

Is it possible to reconcile the economic factors involved in the export control arguments with the national security concerns? The following recommendations try to walk that fine line:

- *Pending completion of the two national studies cited earlier, and in view of the grave national security and law enforcement concerns expressed by government officials, export sales of mass-market software embedded with strong encryption should remain controlled.* Because most relevant mass-market software is currently produced in the United States and is controlled by several other countries as well, there is a reasonable chance that its *widespread* distribution overseas can be controlled for the time being.

- *As one of its specific agenda items, the NRC study of national cryptography policy should assess the national security implications of a phased decontrol of software products with encryption.* The independent panel, consisting of intelligence professionals, specialists from hardware and software companies, and academic experts, should be provided relevant classified information on this matter.

- *When and if the use of these products threatens to become widespread, as it may when foreign suppliers begin to develop products to fill the gap, the United States must be prepared to move promptly on decontrol so that domestic firms are not placed at a competitive disadvantage.*

- *Commerce, not State, should be the lead agency for controlling mass-market software products with encryption.* Routine, automatic approval, however, would not apply to products with strong encryption, nor would such products be subject to findings of "foreign availability" unless such availability is thought to lead to widespread use.[36] This approach will result in a stronger consideration of U.S. business interests in licensing. Provision should be made for NSA to review new technologies, and for State and Defense to be consulted, as appropriate, on exports of potential concern.

- *Requests from U.S. firms to export stand-alone encryption products, with capabilities equivalent to those available overseas, should be routinely granted if it is for the purpose of assisting those firms in establishing secure communications with foreign customers and suppliers.* Requests to supply mass-market business software with strong encryption to key customers should be reviewed on a case-by-case basis.

- *Licenses for the export of key-escrow encryption products in which a U.S. government agency holds a set of keys should be routinely granted.* In this way, strong encryption could be offered with minimal impact on the U.S. intelligence community. Still, there is the obvious question of whether there would be a substantial foreign market for such products.

- *The U.S. government should engage countries with major software producers in discussions about controlling software products with encryption.* Several have intelligence-sharing arrangements with the United States that offer them significant benefit (e.g. UK, Canada, Australia, Israel). Some have export controls as stringent, or even more so, than the United States. For both of these reasons, some of these states may be willing to cooperate on software export controls. This approach is unlikely to do much more than buy time for NSA to adapt its COMINT exploitation efforts for the time when most communications are encrypted. Thus:

- *It is essential that NSA's R&D funding be adequately maintained at a level sufficient to develop new technologies and methods that can mitigate the effects on national security of the inevitable increased use of strong encryption in routine telecommunications.* Emphasis should be placed on preparing for a time when it will become impossible for NSA to monitor a great fraction of foreign communications indiscriminately. Efficient means must be developed to focus COMINT collection assets and code-breaking efforts on the most important communications links.

VI. The Nature Of U.S. Unilateral Controls And Their Implications

U.S. companies often compete under rules that do not apply to their foreign competitors. Such rules include the unilateral controls that the United States imposes on several countries, or entities within countries, for foreign policy reasons. These often prevent exports of commercial items having no military value at all and tend to be highly unpopular within the U.S. business community.[1]

The Export Administration Act gives the President authority "to restrict the export of goods and technology where necessary to further significantly the foreign policy of the United States or to fulfill its declared international obligations."[2] These so-called "foreign policy controls" are concentrated in two areas: anti-terrorism and non-proliferation. Sanctions imposed in support of U.S. anti-terrorist policy seek to apply pressure to states identified by the State Department as sponsors of international terrorism. The states of current concern are Cuba, Iran, Iraq, Libya, North Korea, Syria, and Sudan.[3] Export licenses are required, and routinely denied, for any product or technology that could make a significant contribution to the military potential of these states, including their military logistic capability or ability to conduct terrorism. In the case of Iran, the United States has a mandatory denial policy for *any* export requiring pre-approval.[4] The United States also unilaterally controls exports to states, or organizations within states, known to be involved in weapons proliferation (chemical, biological, or ballistic missile, in addition to nuclear). Sanctions may be applied to foreign entities found to be in violation of relevant U.S. law.

If the United States is a sole supplier of particular items, then it might be argued that unilateral controls could be effective in denying those items to a specific target country. But what if this is not the case? What if the target state can acquire products, equivalent both in quality and quantity, from other willing sources? What good then are unilateral controls? The answer would seem to be "not much." Indeed, there would be no apparent benefit to offset the economic cost in lost sales to U.S. companies.

Others argue that, even in the presence of wide foreign availability, unilateral export controls can play an important role in attaining critical

U.S. foreign policy goals. For example, unilateral controls, even if ineffective in denying trade to targeted states, are symbolic of the principled stands that the United States may be justified in taking as a leader in world affairs. Unilateral sanctions may act to highlight the undesirable behavior of a target state in the eyes of the international community. By conveying resolve, unilateral controls may influence others to cooperate with the United States in seeking the improved behavior of a target state. During an initial period when the United States tries to persuade other suppliers to go along, unilateral controls may be viewed as essential; otherwise, if the United States continues to sell, the credibility of its concern could be undercut. Even if states fail to go along officially, U.S. pressure can dampen the enthusiasm of foreign suppliers to engage in trade in certain items with targeted states.

In this section, we respond to certain of these arguments in considering the implications of unilateral U.S. export controls. Specifically, we examine (1) how U.S. unilateral embargoes affect the manufacturing industry for large, commercial jet aircraft; (2) the issue of unilateral controls implemented under the Enhanced Proliferation Control Initiative (EPCI); and (3) the problem of congressionally mandated unilateral sanctions imposed under the Missile Technology Control Regime (MTCR).

The Iran Embargo: Implications for the U.S. Commercial Aircraft Industry

Under Commerce Department regulations, commercial airliners are exportable without prior approval to most countries, although some components and manufacturing technologies are controlled.[5] The problem is the eight or so countries to which U.S. firms are currently forbidden to sell, a few of which could generate considerable business. The potential sale of twenty Boeing 737s to the government-owned Iran Air is an example of how unilateral controls can create economic costs out of proportion to benefits received.

Aircraft manufacturing generates more export earnings than any other U.S. industry, nearly $29 billion in 1992. The industry comprises two major commercial aircraft makers (Boeing, McDonnell Douglas) and two jet engine builders (General Electric, Pratt & Whitney), and accounts for more than 1.2 million direct and indirect U.S. jobs. The industry is under severe competitive pressure from Europe's Airbus Industrie (a consortium composed of Aerospatiale [France], British Aerospace, Daimler-Benz [Germany] and CASA [Spain]) and will face increasing competition from emerging competitors in Russia and Asia. McDonnell Douglas has lost market share in recent years; both it and Boeing have had significant layoffs of employees.

Because commercial aircraft are low-volume, high-technology goods, firms aggressively exploit every potential market. "First to market" advantages are critical because an initial aircraft purchase by a buyer often generates follow-on orders; the rule of thumb is that the initial sale of one aircraft generates follow-on orders for three more aircraft as well as further sales of spare parts and maintenance services. In some cases the ratio is much higher. Impediments to market access can thus seriously affect future sales. Because of the severe competition, any extraneous factor arising in purchase negotiations can make the difference between a "sale" and "no sale." Direct or indirect government involvement, including subsidies, soft loans, linkages between commercial and defense sales, and export controls can, and do, sway a buyer's decision.

In September 1992, Iran Air signed a tentative contract with Boeing to purchase sixteen 737 aircraft with an option to buy four additional aircraft. The aircraft would be powered by jet engines jointly produced by General Electric and Snecma of France.[6] The deal was subject to the lifting of export restrictions in this specific case by the Commerce Department. Including spare parts, the sale would have generated between $0.8 and $1.0 billion in revenues for Boeing.

The United States considers Iran to be a state sponsor of international terrorism and, as a result, restricts trade in most manufactured goods with Iranian companies. Boeing lobbied for an exception in the case of the Iran Air deal, but was unable to secure a license. Any deal is now unlikely.[7] Several close U.S. allies, including Japan and Germany, still trade in various products with Iran, and Europe's Airbus has considered selling to Iran Air a comparably sized aircraft such as the A320.[8]

A $1 billion loss of revenues to Boeing translates to a loss of about 10,000 "direct" man-years of work for Boeing workers and subcontractors, the great majority of which are in U.S. jobs. Additional job loss would result because the spending generated from each direct man-year yields between one and two "indirect" man-years of work. Every lost sale also leads to a loss of revenue, which decreases the amount of available R&D funds needed to support development of Boeing's next generation aircraft; such development is essential for assuring the viability of Boeing's commercial aircraft product line into the future. Finally, Boeing's loss of this deal means it will also very likely lose future aircraft sales to Iran Air, even if Iran improves its behavior in the interim. Once a major sale is made, the advantage in future sales opportunities resides with the current supplier; the costs of switching often deters a customer from buying from the competition.

However, in cases where Boeing does not get the sale and Airbus does, not all the lost revenue would result in lost U.S. jobs. Indeed, Airbus uses substantial U.S.-built components in its aircraft, ranging from jet engines produced by General Electric to avionics equipment imported from other U.S. firms.[9] Some U.S. suppliers would thus benefit, to a degree, even if Iran Air bought the A320 from Airbus. But the story is more complex. Under U.S. re-export rules, if the dollar value of U.S. controlled components in the A320 aircraft exceeds 10% of the purchase price, Airbus must seek U.S. permission to re-export the American components. This means it must obtain U.S. approval to export the aircraft containing those components. Therefore, to compete in markets that are closed to U.S. firms, Airbus has an incentive to lower its reliance on U.S.-made components below the 10% threshold. In part, this can be accomplished in Airbus-developed aircraft, as in the A330-300, by using British Rolls-Royce rather than U.S. engines. (In the past, the U.S. government, with heavy lobbying by General Electric, authorized the sales of two A300 aircraft to Iran Air precisely to avoid giving Airbus an incentive to "design out" the GE engines.[10]) Even without U.S. engines, however, it is unclear whether U.S. content in the A320 would drop below the 10% threshold. If it did not, and the United States were to deny both Boeing and Airbus from making the Iran Air sale, U.S. component supplier firms would lose—particularly if Iran Air's demand is ultimately met by a third party supplier, such as Russia, which may use no U.S. components at all.[11]

The economic cost of Boeing losing the Iran Air sale is reasonably clear, but what is the benefit? Commercial airliners offer a negligible direct contribution to Iran's military forces.[12] Rather, by the embargo the United States announces to the world that it abhors such actions as Iran's support of international terrorism, witnessed, for example, in the August 1994 bombing of the Jewish Community Center in Buenos Aires and in attacks by Hezbollah terrorists across the Israeli security zone in southern Lebanon, and that it considers Iran a rogue state unworthy of most diplomatic or commercial interaction. But, because U.S. allies have so far declined to join the U.S. dual-use embargo, the real impact falls on U.S. firms. If Boeing does not make the Iran Air sale, but Airbus does (assuming U.S. content is below 10% or a special exception is given to Airbus), Iran will have its airliners and European, not U.S., firms will reap most of the economic gain.

The Boeing-Iran Air example is important because it is one where the economic costs and foreign policy benefits can be brought into reasonably clear focus. Are these unilateral stands worth their economic costs? The answer is "probably not."

A general principle is that the United States should not impose unilateral controls on commercial items for which it is not the sole supplier. Still, at least in the short term, open trade with states such as Iran may be politically infeasible no matter what the rest of the world does. Such situations must be kept to a minimum and all-out efforts must be expended to get all foreign suppliers to go along with U.S. embargoes, ideally before they are imposed. If this fails, specific sales should be permitted when they are clearly in the overall U.S. interest. Approaches other than unilateral export sanctions must be developed to send appropriate messages to irresponsible states. For example, a broader use of controls on imports, particularly when equivalent products are available to U.S. firms from other suppliers, should be considered. Over the long term, however, it will benefit U.S. economic health if purely commercial transactions with international trading partners are viewed not in terms of "friends" and "enemies," but in terms of U.S. economic "interests."

Unilateral Controls Under the Enhanced Proliferation Control Initiative (EPCI)

The most common form of export control requires a company to secure an individual validated license in order to ship dual-use items listed on the Commerce Control List to many foreign destinations. Another form of control, implemented under EPCI, requires a company to secure a license to ship *any* item, whether on the control list or not, if it "knows or is informed" that the end-user for the product is engaged in nuclear, chemical, biological, or missile-related weapons proliferation. This "catch all" provision is designed to block most U.S. exports, including purely commercial items with no military purpose, to end-users engaged in proliferation activities.[13]

The key principle of EPCI is that a firm is responsible for knowing its customers. As currently implemented, however, the "know" rule lacks clarity and does not provide companies with clear criteria for action. If an illegal transfer occurs, however, company officers are subject to civil and criminal penalties.[14] Because the burden of proof rests with company officials to explain how they acted in good faith in determining that a license was not needed for a specific end-user, EPCI breeds an overly cautious approach in which a license is sought in many cases where it is not needed. The inherent delays in this process work to the competitive disadvantage of U.S. firms and can even be a disincentive to legitimate exports.[15]

There are other problems with the EPCI catch-all rule. For example, it was intended to apply only to those items that could make a "material contribution" to developing WMDs and associated delivery systems—its practical effect has been to prohibit transfers of most goods to suspicious end users. "Material contribution" is difficult to define for many technologies. Is it that which is *required* to design, build, or deliver a WMD, or merely that which is *useful*? In December 1993 the Commerce Department's Bureau of Export Administration tried to clarify the EPCI guidelines along the following lines: A U.S. exporter must apply for a license if it knows or is informed that an item will "be directly employed" or "directly assist" in the "design, development, production, stockpiling, or use of missiles or CBW . . .".[16] This clarification, while an improvement, still fails to define which specific items will "directly assist" development of WMD.

The rule imposes significant added administrative costs and burdens, particularly on small firms. Those engaged in purely commercial activities, whose products heretofore had not come under controls, are now required to establish an export administration infrastructure. In certain cases, this has provided a disincentive for small firms to export their products.

Few other states control non-critical items to destinations of proliferation concern. An exception is Germany, which has added a similar catch-all provision to its new, tighter export control laws.[17] Also, after considerable debate, the European Union (EU) has recently adopted a catch-all rule, as yet still not implemented, which is weaker than that of Germany or the United States. The rule applies to products and technologies not listed on the EU dual-use list in cases, for example, where an "exporter has been informed by his authorities" that such items may be used in connection with WMD or missile development programs.[18] Other key suppliers of high-technology items in Europe and Asia do not even have this less-restrictive rule. Because it is not multilateral, the EPCI catch-all rule is unlikely to be effective. Moreover, even if our CoCom partners and other key suppliers applied the U.S.'s more restrictive rule, "front" organizations could be set up within states to import commercial items and divert them to proscribed end-users.

The U.S. government does not provide organized assistance, such as through its intelligence agencies, to help firms identify foreign end-users engaged in proliferation. Industry would like the government to publish "watch lists" of proscribed destinations, but this may not be practical given the intelligence community's concerns about protecting sensitive sources and methods of intelligence collection. Even if it were, there is still a distributor problem: often firms sell products via independent distributor networks and have little control over where those products eventually get shipped; they rely on the distributors to obtain the necessary licenses.

In its recent report, the Office of Technology Assessment provides a useful framework for considering this problem.[19] It developed options to ease the burden of EPCI on industry including (1) eliminate the catch-all rule by having Commerce list "*all* the products for which an export license is required and all the countries and specific end-users as well", (2) maintain the rule but make clear to firms that they will not be required "to probe deeply into the character of end-users of relatively innocuous products," (3) change the "knows or is informed rule" to an "is informed" rule, and (4) maintain the rule, but publish a specific list of controllable items.

We argue that the EPCI catch-all rule as currently cast should be substantially revised or, failing that, eliminated. The difficulties associated with its current implementation do not seem worth the costs; other mechanisms must be found to pressure proscribed end-users rather than to cease trading in items having no real relationship to WMDs. Nor is it practical for the United States to attempt to make the rule widely multilateral; there are simply too many foreign suppliers who would be unwilling to go along. At the very least the rule should be revised to bring it into accord with the "is informed" language adopted by the EU, and a list of items that "directly assist" WMD programs should be published. This approach might also be more acceptable to other supplier states in Europe and Asia contemplating a catch-all rule. If the EPCI rule is retained, company officials should be presumed to act in good faith unless clear evidence indicates otherwise. They would thus be protected when items are exported to end-users not known by them to be involved in proliferation activity. This increases incentives for companies to export their products.

Unilateral U.S. Sanctions Under the MTCR

The United States strictly interprets its commitments under the MTCR. Unlike that of any of its other MTCR partners, U.S. law requires the President to impose punitive trade sanctions against foreign or domestic firms that export to non-MTCR states the systems, components, or technologies used in missile development, production, and deployment. Once a determination is made that an illegal transfer has occurred, the President, under current law, has little flexibility to decide whether or not to apply, sanctions.[20] At times, U.S. mandatory sanctions policy has cut against other U.S. foreign policy goals and economic interests. Two examples are noteworthy.

The Russian space agency Glavkosmos concluded a contract to sell liquid rocket engines and associated production technologies to the civilian Indian Space Research Organization (ISRO). Both parties stated that the equipment was to be used only for peaceful purposes in India's space launch program. In May 1992, the United States imposed trade sanctions on Glavkosmos and ISRO, claiming that the impending sale was in violation of the MTCR. In July 1993, after intensive negotiations and under great pressure from the United States, the sanctions were lifted when President Yeltsin agreed not to transfer liquid engine production technology to India, although several of the engines themselves are being shipped at substantial profit. In return, the United States promised Russia potentially lucrative cooperation in civilian space activities.

U.S. sanctions were applied during a period of increasing political and economic chaos in Russia. There was, and continues to be, a strong U.S. national security interest in promoting political stabilization and economic transformation in Russia. The United States also has been working hard to encourage Russian firms involved in defense production to convert to peaceful application. In both of these regards the hundreds of millions of dollars that Glavkosmos stood to gain from the ISRO deal would have been of great benefit. That the United States, under its mandatory sanctions policy, "went to the mat" to punish this sale (and caused Yeltsin to expend political capital to overturn the original contract) worked to undercut other vital and perhaps more pressing U.S. interests.

In August 1993, in response to the alleged transfer of M-11 missile components to Pakistan, the United States imposed so-called "Category II" trade sanctions on China's Ministry of Aerospace Industry and its subsidiaries.[21] The Chinese government denied that an illegal transfer to Pakistan occurred, disputed the U.S. claim that the M-11 exceeded the range-payload limit established under the MTCR, bitterly denounced the sanctions, and later threatened to abandon its earlier commitment to adhere to the MTCR.

The M-11 sanctions, if implemented fully, would have had a substantial economic impact on U.S. companies, making it more difficult if not impossible for some U.S. aerospace firms to conclude deals involving the export of satellite systems to China for launch. As it has turned out, a waiver was granted in January 1994 that permitted certain U.S. satellites to be launched by China.[22] And, by October 1994, after difficult negotiations, the Clinton administration reached an accord in which it lifted the sanctions in return for China's renewed adherence to the MTCR, including a pledge not to transfer MTCR-constrained missile systems to Pakistan.[23]

At a time when China's economy is booming, the M-11 sanctions placed U.S. companies intent on entering new and potentially lucrative Chinese markets at great disadvantage in regard to the foreign competition. Further, the sanctions were imposed shortly after a highly charged U.S. political debate over China's human-rights violations and the granting of most-favored-nation trading status. The sanctions have contributed significantly to a deterioration in U.S.-China relations precisely during a period when the United States needed China's help on a critical matter. Specifically, China is key to efforts to roll back North Korea's nuclear weapons program, for example, in the ongoing diplomacy surrounding the implementation of the U.S.-DPRK Framework Agreement of October 21, 1994. The United States risked undercutting this critical goal by punishing

China over the important yet secondary concern of Pakistan's missile proliferation.

These examples show the importance that the United States places on controlling missile proliferation, even when unilateral and mandatory sanctions come in conflict with other U.S. goals and interests. But is the United States carefully taking into account the costs and benefits of this policy? In weighing several factors, including an assessment of the military utility of missiles in comparison with other strike systems, we argue that unilateral and mandatory MTCR sanctions are not in the overall U.S. interest. Rather, a strong case can be made for giving the President more flexibility and discretion in employing sanctions, including the flexibility to modify, postpone, or suspend sanctions consonant with other pressing U.S. foreign policy objectives.

The version of the Export Administration Act of 1994 proposed by the administration provided the President with the flexibility to delay sanctions for up to 180 days under certain circumstances.[24] Flexibility is also increased by eliminating the current "Category I violation" mandatory sanction (two years denial of individual validated export licenses for all items on the Commerce Control List) and giving the President the discretion to impose a broader range of sanctions depending on the specific circumstances.[25] These are small steps in the right direction and should be sustained in Congressional deliberations regarding a new EAA.

Recommendations:

- *In general, the United States should not impose unilateral controls on commercial items for which it is not the sole supplier.* If other key suppliers do not go along, then controls will be both ineffective and costly to U.S. firms. Before imposing an embargo, therefore, the United States must exert strong efforts to seek multilateral participation.

- *If imposed for overriding political reasons, unilateral controls should be accompanied with "sunset provisions" that go into effect after a fixed period of time unless the controls have become multilateral.* The President, of course, should have the flexibility either to allow or to ban specific exports to specific end-users when dictated by overriding national security/economic interests.

- *Substantive reviews of U.S. unilateral controls should be conducted semi-annually.*

- *The United States should examine whether a broader use of denying imports from targeted states, or organizations within states, might be warranted, particularly when equivalent products are available to the U.S. from other sources.*

- *Substantially revise the EPCI "catch-all" rule. Failing that, eliminate it.* It does not seem practical that diplomatic efforts could succeed in making the current rule widely multilateral. An "is informed" rule similar to the European Union could be instituted, and a list published of all items that "directly assist" WMD development. In creating this list, "foreign availability" should be a factor. Such an approach would be more acceptable to other supplier states in Europe and Asia contemplating a catch-all rule. If the "know" part of the EPCI rule is retained, draft clear criteria for how well a firm must know its customers, and apply a presumption-of-innocence standard when investigating questionable transfers. Devote intelligence resources to help firms identify end-users engaged in proliferation.

- *Provide the President more flexibility in imposing sanctions under the MTCR.* Initial steps should be along the lines of Section 12A of the President's proposed EAA of 1994.

VII. Conclusions And Recommendations

Export controls will continue to be a tool in U.S. national security policy, but generally one of declining value. Rapid economic and political change, including the trend toward global diffusion of high-technology, are making it more difficult to achieve multilateral consensus on controls. CoCom, once the West's bulwark against technology flow to communist countries, has gone away and its replacement is likely to be substantially weaker and oriented only towards the proliferation threat.

Controls must focus on the most pressing problems—the proliferation of nuclear, chemical, and biological weapons—and less on trying to control, as did CoCom, a broad range of high technology. It is much more important to devote limited resources to control critical items such as plutonium and highly enriched uranium, and the means for producing these materials.

A comprehensive approach to U.S. export control reform must answer the following questions:

- What are the specific post-Cold War U.S. national security and foreign policy goals?
- What is the U.S. national defense strategy for achieving them?
- What is the role of advanced technology in U.S. national defense?
- How can export controls on high-technology best advance U.S. national security, for example, by denying significant military capability to potential adversaries?
- What are the resulting economic costs and impacts to U.S. companies?
- How are the changes in the global marketplace in high-technology products affecting the utility and effectiveness of export controls?

These are broad questions and this paper only touches on certain aspects of them. But we have illustrated key points with several examples. We conclude by summarizing the recommendations that have emerged from our study. Some are currently being debated as Congress and the administration seek to reach consensus on legislation for export control reform.

On Computers and Microprocessors:

- *Controls on computers at the 10-1000 Mtops range or above are unlikely to impede emerging nuclear weapons programs.* Our analysis thus supports the recent relaxation of lower-end computer controls.

- *Some controls on supercomputers, those having performance levels at the current state of the art (10,000-100,000 Mtops and above), will continue to be in the U.S. interest.* It is the "true" supercomputers that provide the greatest leverage in maintaining the U.S. lead in advanced defense technology. Export control thresholds could be set one or two orders of magnitude below the state-of-the-art systems currently in use by the U.S. defense industry and the Intelligence Community.

- *Indexing should be adopted to allow for timely, coordinated decontrol of microprocessors and computers prior to their becoming available from foreign sources that do not implement appropriate export controls.* An expert advisory panel could facilitate oversight. In no case should the United States continue to control a computer for which the associated microprocessor is generally available. The concern is that such microprocessors can be incorporated in foreign-made clones that (1) are exported without control, or (2) do not require U.S. re-export authorization because the value of the microprocessor does not exceed the de minimus threshold. Such a situation is highly disadvantageous to U.S. companies. Special microprocessors developed for military applications, including radiation-hardened versions, would remain subject to controls.

- *Export controls should be fully lifted on microprocessors now under general commercial distribution or where the production technology is widely licensed abroad.* Sun's current SPARC line, Intel's x86 series (including the Pentium), and the newly released

PowerPC chips exemplify processors requiring export licenses to certain destinations. Because there is no effective way to monitor or control microprocessor exports, continued regulation imposes an anti-competitive burden on U.S. exporters. A limited category of the most advanced U.S. microprocessors could continue to be controlled, but only if U.S. firms remain sole source suppliers and product quantities remain limited. High-end chips produced for the multiprocessor workstation market might fit this category. As the development of massively parallel systems progresses, however, it will become easier for users to tackle computing problems by linking together a very large number of less powerful chips. This technique will eventually make controls on even the highest performance microprocessors impractical.

- *The U.S. government should take a fresh look at the national security and economic costs and benefits of transferring abroad potentially sensitive technology and know-how for the manufacture of dual-use, high-technology products, including microprocessors.* Items manufactured abroad with U.S.-licensed technology cannot be controlled as effectively as in the United States. Furthermore, the dissemination of such knowledge naturally strengthens indigenous capabilities for manufacture. The choice between denying exports of manufacturing technologies (at the expense of the commercial interests of U.S. firms), or promulgating them under conditions that make controls infeasible, requires a thoughtful cost-benefit analysis in each case.

- *Antiquated controls on transfers of technical or proprietary data should be relaxed in the case of U.S. firms trying to engage in cooperative R&D ventures with commercial partners in the former Soviet bloc.* Caution must still be exercised because of the potential that such information could be used in military programs, but we expect that the potential downside in this regard would be small for many of the ventures involving collaboration in basic research. In many cases, the transfer of data of real significance produced in the venture is one-way into the United States.

- *Continue export controls on specialized encryption chips and related hardware as mandated under the ITARs.* Pay particularly close attention to export license requests for large shipments of these devices.

On Mass-Market Software with Encryption:

- *Pending completion of the two national studies cited earlier, and in view of the grave national security and law enforcement concerns expressed by government officials, export sales of mass-market software embedded with strong encryption should remain controlled.* Because most relevant mass-market software is currently produced in the United States and is controlled by several other countries as well, there is a reasonable chance that its *widespread* distribution overseas can be controlled for the time being.

- *As one of its specific agenda items, the NRC study of national cryptography policy should assess the national security implications of a phased decontrol of software products with encryption.* The independent panel, consisting of intelligence professionals, specialists from hardware and software companies, and academic experts, should be provided relevant classified information on this matter.

- *When and if the use of these products threatens to become widespread, as it may when foreign suppliers begin to develop products to fill the gap, the United States must be prepared to move promptly on decontrol so that domestic firms are not placed at a competitive disadvantage.*

- *Commerce, not State, should be the lead agency for controlling mass-market software products with encryption.* Routine, automatic approval, however, would not apply to products with strong encryption, nor would such products be subject to findings of "foreign availability" unless such availability is thought to lead to widespread use. This approach will result in a stronger consideration of U.S. business interests in licensing. Provision should be made for NSA to review new technologies, and for State and Defense to be consulted, as appropriate, on exports of potential concern.

- *Requests from U.S. firms to export stand-alone encryption products, with capabilities equivalent to those available overseas, should be routinely granted if it is for the purpose of assisting those firms in establishing secure communications with foreign customers and suppliers.* Requests to supply mass-market business software with strong encryption to key customers should be reviewed on a case-by-case basis.

- *Licenses for the export of key-escrow encryption products in which a U.S. government agency holds a set of keys should be routinely granted.* In this way, strong encryption could be offered with minimal impact on the U.S. intelligence community. Still, there is the obvious question of whether there would be a substantial foreign market for such products.

- *The U.S. government should engage countries with major software producers in discussions about controlling software products with encryption.* Several have intelligence sharing arrangements with the United States that offer them significant benefit (e.g., United Kingdom, Canada, Australia, Israel). Some have export controls as stringent, or even more so, than the United States. For both of these reasons, some of these states may be willing to cooperate on software export controls. This approach, however, is unlikely to do much more than buy time for NSA to adapt its COMINT exploitation efforts for the time when most communications are encrypted. Thus:

- *It is essential that NSA's R&D funding be adequately maintained at a level sufficient to develop new technologies and methods that can mitigate the effects on national security of the inevitable increased use of strong encryption in routine telecommunications.* Emphasis should be placed on preparing for a time when it will become impossible for NSA to monitor a great fraction of foreign communications indiscriminately. Efficient means must be developed to focus COMINT collection assets and code-breaking work on the most important communications links.

On U.S. Unilateral Controls:

- *In general, the United States should not impose unilateral controls on commercial items for which it is not the sole supplier.* If other key suppliers do not go along, then controls will be both ineffective and costly to U.S. firms. Before imposing an embargo, therefore, the United States must exert strong efforts to seek multilateral participation.

- *If imposed for overriding political reasons, unilateral controls should be accompanied with "sunset provisions" that go into effect after a fixed period of time unless the controls have become multilateral.* The President, of course, should have the flexibility either to allow or to ban specific exports to specific end-users when dictated by overriding national security/economic interests.

- *Substantive reviews of U.S. unilateral controls should be conducted semi-annually.*

- *The United States should examine whether a broader use of denying imports from targeted states, or organizations within states, might be warranted, particularly when equivalent products are available to the United States from other sources.*

- *Substantially revise the EPCI "catch-all" rule. Failing that, eliminate it.* It does not seem practical that diplomatic efforts could succeed in making the current rule widely multilateral. An "is informed" rule similar to the European Union could be instituted, and a list published of all items that "directly assist" WMD development. In creating this list, "foreign availability" should be a factor. Such an approach would be more acceptable to other supplier states in Europe and Asia contemplating a catch-all rule. If the "know" part of the EPCI rule is retained, draft clear criteria for how well a firm must know its customers, and apply a presumption of innocence standard when investigating questionable transfers. Devote intelligence resources to help firms identify end-users engaged in proliferation.

- *Provide the President more flexibility in imposing sanctions under the MTCR.* Initial steps should be along the lines of Section 12A of the President's proposed EAA of 1994.

On General Export Control Matters:

- *Assess the economic impact of controls.* Proposals to strengthen controls on existing items, or add new controls, should include statements detailing how the controls will affect the market share and competitiveness of U.S. firms, and the economic costs, including job losses. This should be done with existing controls as well.

- *Apply controls discriminately, with much greater attention to foreign availability.* Concentrate efforts on outlaw states. Policies must be flexible so they can be adjusted when a state's behavior improves or worsens. Controls are not only useless as a policy tool but harmful to U.S. firms if they are unilateral and not adequately enforceable.

- *In implementing controls in general, consider not only the technology itself but the degree to which specific states can exploit it to develop WMD or threaten the U.S. lead in advanced conventional arms or in code breaking.* There are only a few states in the world considered potentially hostile to the United States who are able to exploit high technology to create, for example, an indigenous reconnaissance-strike force, or a capability to counter one. For those who are unable, the best approach is not so much to worry about their acquisition of high technology, but to convince suppliers of advanced weapons systems not to sell to them.

- *Implement prenotification of exports.* Even as controls are relaxed, companies should continue to prenotify their exports so that data is available concerning what advanced technologies, materials, and equipment goes where. This would permit a firm to be advised informally about a potentially damaging transfer and would also help the intelligence community track proliferant activity.

- *Clarify and simplify the export control regulations.*

In the long term, "supply side" measures will not stop determined states from acquiring WMD; the United States must plan to mitigate their military impact when vital national interests are at stake. A prudent "counter proliferation" effort is necessary, but need not, as critics suggest, detract from "non-proliferation" policies.

The United States must also continue to advance specific approaches to reduce demand for these weapons, taking the lead in advancing political solutions to security concerns and conflict in regions such as the Middle

East, South Asia, and the Korean peninsula. Over the long term, effective regional security arrangements are the only sure way to remove the threat that these enormously destructive weapons will one day be used.

Finally, U.S. national security and economic security are inexorably linked. Sensible export control reform will not provide adversaries with advanced weapons to kill American men and women in combat, but can help create the conditions for a more prosperous and secure United States.

Appendix I. The U.S. Export Control System Simplified

U.S. exports are controlled for three specific reasons: national security, foreign policy, or the short supply of a commodity within the United States. Legislation pending before Congress that would reform the Export Administration Act (the basic source of U.S. authority to regulate exports) will not alter this fundamental focus. In most instances, Congress has authorized executive branch discretion when imposing export controls, unless they are mandated by a specific act. The Nuclear Non-Proliferation Act of 1978, for instance, provides for the control of exports of nuclear technology that could support the development or manufacture of nuclear explosives. Other mandatory controls are imposed on state sponsors of international terrorism.

Comprising an important subcategory that overlaps traditional national security and foreign policy rationales are export controls geared to stop the spread of weapons of mass destruction (WMD). Non-proliferation controls regulate trade in components and technology relevant to nuclear, chemical, and biological weapons, and missile delivery systems.

All U.S. commercial and defense exports require a license. The United States also restricts exports to all destinations, unlike its major allies who traditionally impose far fewer controls on commercial exports to non-communist and post-communist states. The United States tends to view exporting more as a "privilege" than a "right." This has been the source of much friction with allies in Europe and Asia, who continue to trade with countries such as Iran, which is embargoed by the United States. A complication is that the United States tries to control the export or "re-export" of products or technology originating in the United States, but which are re-shipped to a third party from a foreign country. Often, foreign-based exporters must obtain prior U.S. permission to re-export such goods.

Most products can be shipped without government certification or paperwork under the broad grant of authority known as a general license. Commercial goods requiring approval prior to shipment or re-export are regulated by the Commerce Department's Bureau of Export Administration (BXA).[1] The State Department controls the export of arms and other weaponry through the Munitions List (as governed by the Arms Export Control Act of 1976). A limited number of goods are regulated by other departments. The Nuclear Regulatory Commission (NRC), for example, controls the export of nuclear power reactors.

The United States also participates in several multilateral regimes, the most important of which has long been CoCom, the Coordinating Committee for Multilateral Export Controls. CoCom was responsible for the regulation of trade to the former Communist bloc, but it expired March 31, 1994 by agreement of its members in response to the end of the Cold War. A follow-on regime (tentatively known as the "New Forum") is currently being negotiated. In addition to this eventual successor to CoCom, there are four other major multilateral export control arrangements in which the United States participates. These are the Nuclear Non-Proliferation regime, the Missile Technology Control Regime (MTCR), the Australia Group (which seeks to limit the spread of chemical and biological weapons), and the bilateral U.S.-Japanese Supercomputer accord (which U.S. negotiators have tried unsuccessfully to expand).

As noted above, U.S. regulations governing dual-use exports are based upon the Export Administration Act or EAA.[2] This act authorizes Commerce to establish and maintain the Export Administration Regulations (EAR).[3] Although the EAR is designed principally to implement the EAA, it also serves to implement other related acts regulating the export of products from the United States. For example, the EAR covers dual-use nuclear-related items, missile technology not controlled by the State Department, and the export of crude oil. The EAR contains the Commerce Control List (CCL) on which is found all items controlled for export by the United States except those exclusively under the jurisdiction of another government agency.[4]

It is the exporter's responsibility to determine which department or agency controls a particular product and to obtain the necessary license. Typically, this will be the Commerce Department, which regulates overseas trade in most dual-use goods. The export control status of any particular good must then be determined by a combination of three factors: (1) the item's technical characteristics (2) whether it is equipment, a material, production-related, information, or software; and (3) the item's export destination. The burden for most commercial exporters is:

- Determining the proper Commerce license category for a product;

- Obtaining Commerce pre-approval, if required, to ship a specified product to a particular destination; and

- Being informed, under the Enhanced Proliferation Control Initiative (EPCI), of whether a product's end-user is involved in proliferation activities.

EPCI was announced by President Bush in December 1990. It requires that firms acquire government approval to export products of any kind to a destination that they "either know or are informed" is engaged in WMD proliferation. In essence, EPCI strengthened U.S. export control efforts by holding exporters liable for shipments to suspected proliferants, even when such exports would not ordinarily require prior approval.

For all exporters, the most important distinction to make is between items requiring government pre-approval prior to export and items that do not—which is less obvious than it sounds. Exporters must also keep in mind that while a given product's characteristics may place it beneath the control threshold for some countries, hence making it "decontrolled," the same item may still be "controlled" to a number of other locations. Based upon these general distinctions, Commerce has designated two main license categories: "general" and "validated." Most goods can be shipped under a "general destination" or G-Dest license and thus require no prior written approval to export. A significant percentage of high-technology items, however, do require pre-approval and must be exported under a validated license.

There are a number of special general licenses that essentially provide an exemption to validated licensing requirements. Currently, the most important of these are "general free world" or GFW, "general CoCom trade" or GCT, and "general limited value" or GLV.[5] GFW allows items to be shipped without prior approval to many free world countries.[6] GLV is a similar license, but used only to make small-scale shipments of certain goods not exceeding a limited value. GCT allows exports of most dual-use items to other members of CoCom without the need for prior approval. Finally, with the dissolution of CoCom, Commerce established a new general license GLX to authorize certain exports to civilian end-users (and for end-uses) in states that were formerly proscribed. Under GLX, for instance, U.S. manufacturers can ship personal computers and workstations long banned for export to formerly proscribed destinations in Russia.

Appendix II. Implications Of The Microprocessor For Supercomputing

Computational capability is now largely inseparable from the microprocessor—a technology that may be the critical link in the evolution of even more powerful computers.[1] Certainly, mainframe producers are aware of the dramatic impact that processor-based systems have had on the computer industry. Their declining market results from the ability to pack mainframe-size computer power onto a single thumbnail-size chip. Costing only a few hundred dollars apiece, the microprocessor has generated a mass commercial market.

Today, as this report argues, semiconductor manufacturing is global and U.S. microprocessor designs are widely disseminated abroad. PCs and workstations can be assembled from component parts in dozens of locations around the world. Software advances also allow various microprocessors of comparable performance to be substitutable, such that IBM software can run on a PowerPC chip. Chips may thus become commodities where brands compete on price, performance, and marketing.[2]

Current trends relating to parallel computing systems suggest that it is ultimately futile to expect export controls to continue to restrain the spread of high-performance computing. Parallel computers are those that use two or more central processing units (CPU) to solve a single problem by working in tandem.[3] There are two types: multiprocessors, which use only a limited number of CPUs (working together or separately), and massively parallel processors (MPP), which are scalable and can potentially link together several thousand or more inexpensive microprocessors. MPP-based supercomputers may ultimately achieve performance levels that are orders of magnitude above the most advanced traditional supercomputers. But development and use of MPP systems has been slowed both by the architectural complexity of linking so many chips and the challenge of writing software that best exploits their features.[4]

Still, the supercomputer industry, as the mainframe industry before it, is losing market share to producers of far less expensive multiprocessor workstations, which are capable of performing many tasks once only suited to the world's fastest machines.[5] If the hardware and software problems are solved, the use of advanced microprocessors, which are relatively cheap, widely available, and, hence, uncontrollable, will allow designers from around the world to build powerful multiprocessors or even MPP systems. Hence, in 1992, India, which has been denied access to U.S. supercomputers, developed a relatively sophisticated parallel system using low-performance microprocessors readily obtained on the world market.[6]

The emerging commercial significance of multiprocessor architectures is indicated by the efforts of U.S. companies such as Silicon Graphics (SGI) and Sun Microsystems. SGI is developing advanced parallel systems that it expects will become the core components for on-demand, video distribution systems. To meet this goal, SGI has formed multimedia joint ventures with Japan's Nippon Telegraph and Telephone Corporation and AT&T, and is currently jointly field testing a system with Time Warner.[7] Formerly, only traditional supercomputers could attain a volume and rate of data access needed to perform such a computing task. In fact, SGI compares its newest offerings (the SGI Power Challenge line) to the Cray Y-MP family. SGI's top-rated 18-processor system (starting at $165K) achieves a performance of 5.4 Gflops. The company has received hundreds of orders from firms all over the world, even though customers must wait 18 months for delivery.[8]

Sun is also working to enhance and expand the multiprocessing features of its present and future SPARC workstations. To facilitate this, it has even employed some of Russia's best supercomputer and parallel software designers, and, in the process, has broken new ground in dealing with the complexities of U.S. export controls (See Appendix III). Efforts such as these suggest the magnitude of the potential market anticipated by these firms for parallel systems, which some observers expect will eventually supplant much of the market for traditional supercomputers.[9]

Current export controls on the highest performance computers have focused on supercomputer mainframe systems produced in the United States and Japan. As MPP development advances, and progress is made in solving the complex problems in architecture and software design, we should anticipate that most computing problems will be able to be tackled by these systems, rather than by relying on a few of the most advanced CPUs. It may be that the days of effective export controls on computing at the highest performance levels are numbered.

Appendix III. Export Controls And Sun Microsystems In Russia

Cameron Binkley and Elaine Naugle

Sun Microsystems Inc., a Fortune 500 company headquartered in California, is the world's largest UNIX-based computer workstation manufacturer. Sun ranked 29th in total 1993 sales of U.S. merchandise exports, with a significant fraction of its earnings derived from export income.[1] In 1992 and 1993, Sun began expanding its operations into Russia, involving itself both in the distribution of computer hardware and the initiation of two R&D projects intended to further Sun's work in advanced microprocessor design, software development, and wireless communications technology. In one effort, Sun has collaborated with a highly skilled team of Russian engineers from a premier high-technology development organization—the Moscow Center for SPARC Technology (MCST).[2] This case study focuses on how U.S. Cold War-era restrictions on the transfer of sophisticated dual-use products and technology have affected Sun's venture with MCST.[3]

Sun's Russian Projects and U.S. Export Controls

The U.S. government has had several concerns regarding the transfer of technology from Sun to its Russian partners. Although the immediate threat of superpower military confrontation has dramatically declined, the future of U.S.-Russian relations is anything but certain. Therefore, the United States has sought to maintain its overall right to control militarily relevant technology transfers to Russia. The growing outflow of sensitive Russian technology also implies to U.S. officials a limited capacity by Russia and Russian firms to guarantee compliance with U.S. controls on the subsequent transfer of such goods to third countries.

When Sun began its Russian effort, U.S. government concern over the former involvement of Sun's Russian employees in secret military projects, and the possibility that the company's technology might eventually find its way back into the Russian military,[4] left Sun's export license applications lost in limbo for more than a year. U.S. concern over the export of encryption software and the possibility that such a prospect would reduce the ability of the United States to gather foreign intelligence has also led to licensing complications.

Sun-Russian Cooperative Development Efforts

MCST was formed as private commercial company. It was spun off from a larger defense industry organization known as the Institute for Precision Mechanics and Computer Technology (ITMVT). MCST is not a subsidiary of Sun, but a partner that Sun supports. Sun contracts with MCST instead of paying salaries.

The chairman of MCST's board of directors is Boris Babaian, a figure who is sometimes compared to Seymour Cray, the famed U.S. supercomputer designer. Russia's changing political and economic conditions inspired Babaian to seek out Western commercial contracts, including Sun, whose technology he believed was highly compatible with what was being developed in his own institute. The formation of MCST has allowed Babaian to cope with scaled back government funding, making it possible for him to continue employing his engineering team while furthering the stalled development of Russia's most advanced computer—and Babaian's main project—the Elbrus III.[5]

Sun has sought to engage MCST's unique talent pool to further the design and software development of its world-renowned SPARC engineering workstations.[6] SPARC, which stands for Scalable Processor Architecture, is Sun's trademark for the microprocessors that characterize Sun systems. SPARC technology is commercially significant because of its ability to utilize or adapt to various types of multiprocessor media, handling features that demand ever-greater speed—an important edge in the highly competitive workstation market.[7]

In fact, Babaian's supercomputer experience is highly relevant to Sun. Manufacturing advances in the miniaturization of semiconductors now allow top designers to apply supercomputer engineering and software techniques to mass-market microprocessors.[8] The key to the Sun-MCST relationship is the fact that inferior Russian semiconductor manufacturing technology has forced Russian supercomputer designers to generate software engineering solutions that are more ingenious than those devised by Western firms with access to superior production technology.[9] The Elbrus III, for instance, achieves Cray-comparable performance using well-written software to overcome hardware that is far behind Western standards.[10]

Simply said, Babaian is well-placed to help Sun push past current limits in developing software and circuit designs for faster microprocessors. (See related discussion in Section IV.)

In addition to its work with Sun, MCST is negotiating with other Western companies and has explored the possibility of doing business with Asian firms, few of which are hampered by export control concerns. For example, MCST has contacted South Korea's Samsung, marketing itself as a high-technology design house for products that other firms could build.[11] Finally, MCST distributes computers in Russia for Sun and other Western firms.

MCST offers outstanding design skills, but lacks the technology to manufacture products competitive in the West or Russia. It has found a natural ally in Sun. Beyond mining MCST's engineering and programming talents, Sun benefits by the substantially lower cost of employing Russians.[12]

Delays and Restrictions in Licensing Process

Sun's MCST venture has been successful, but export controls demand persistent effort. Sun's first major problem involved getting U.S. government permission to conduct joint research in a project where much of the technology remains controlled. For instance, it took Sun more than twelve months to obtain its original license for working with MCST. Table 8 below describes the chronology of steps taken for Sun's MCST license. Throughout the twelve-month period, Sun was involved in a constant dialogue with several government agencies involved with reviewing the license, a complexity that seriously delayed the process. Change in political administrations and insufficiently knowledgeable government licensing staff may have caused even further delays.

The license finally issued for MCST was extremely restrictive. Sun was not permitted to provide design, manufacturing technology, controlled technical data, or assistance for microprocessors or computers above the 12.5 CTP level. Nor could Sun aid MCST in writing software used to help develop computers. Of course, the re-export from Russia of any MCST-developed product using Sun technology was also controlled.[13]

Sun was allowed to export some microprocessor software and software development tools such as various design compilers and SPARC test vectors. Two logic design projects were also approved, but these were constrained because Sun's license requires the company to provide no more than "go/no-go" responses when contacted for direction by MCST. Moreover, further licenses were needed to engage in any conversations beyond these narrow definitions. This subject is addressed in greater detail below.

1992	
April 24	Sun's MCST export license request submitted to Commerce
May 20	License referred to Defense Technology Security Agency (DTSA)
May - August	Series of DTSA questions on all phases of MCST project
August 17	Sun officials fly to Washington to answer DTSA questions; Presentations given to DTSA, Navy, Air Force, Naval Research Labs, and State
September	DTSA requests that Sun provide full list of equipment that will be given to MCST; Sun argues that research projects cannot easily specify future project needs
October 12	Sun officials to Washington again for meetings with DTSA, State, and Commerce to answer more questions
1993	
January - April	Sun must re-communicate to new administration facts of case and technology involved with MCST license
	Sun engages in constant negotiations with DTSA over license
	DTSA sends license to Operating Committee, an interagency group
	Operating Committee escalates license to Advisory Committee ACEP, second interagency group
April	Newly appointed Defense team approves conditions at ACEP
April 27	Commerce issues extremely restricted license

Source: Luke Alexander, Sun Microsystems, February 1995.

Table 8: Sun-MCST License Approval Chronology

Export Controls on Computers

A series of liberalizations, which peaked in March 1994, dramatically relaxed controls on the export of computers to Russia and other former East bloc countries. Prior to this decontrol, Sun could not send its most advanced workstations to MCST (nor could it market these in Russia). U.S. approval was required for any computer running at 12.5 Mtops or above, roughly equivalent to a slower-running 486-based machine.[14] Thus, Sun's Russian subsidiaries had to operate without essential equipment because the company was prohibited from transferring workstations more powerful than a Sparcstation 1+.[15] This significantly obstructed MCST in its attempt to help Sun design an advanced microprocessor.[16] Today, the performance threshold for computers exported to civilian end-users in the former Soviet Union is 1000 Mtops.

During the period that Sun's computer exports to Russia were restricted, a Taiwanese computer company named Tatung, which manufactures SPARC station clones, was selling comparable, but uncontrolled, equipment across the street from MCST in Moscow.[17] Tatung's machines are made with SPARC microprocessors, which, though they were not supposed to be available in machines sold to such countries as Russia, have long been easily obtained throughout the non-Communist world. Because Taiwan was not then party to any Western export control regime, the firm was able to set up in Russia (and China), completely unencumbered by any kind of export restrictions. Tatung even had the habit of calling the MCST office to sell it Tatung's version of Sun's SPARC computers! MCST could not purchase these, of course, as this would have constituted a deliberate circumvention of U.S. law.[18]

While the U.S. government has lifted restrictions on most personal computers and workstations that are exported to Russian non-military enterprises, certain restrictions on other types of hardware and software remain. A continuing administrative headache is the need for Sun to assure itself of legal compliance prior to shipping even non-controlled parts to Russia.[19] Finally, as examined more closely below, U.S. export restrictions continue to hamper Sun's ability to conduct technically related project discussions with Russian engineers.

Export Controls on Technical Discussions

Sun's export license with MCST restricts any type of technical discussion that is not pre-approved by the U.S. government. Specifically, Sun is restricted from providing any "controlled technical data/assistance concerning design implementation, corrections or improvements for any of the hardware or software design projects."[20] The Commerce Department defines "technical data" as the actual shipment, transmission, or release of technical information (also meaning "technology" or "technical assistance") to foreign nationals through written, visual, or oral means, or the application abroad of personal technical knowledge acquired in the United States.[21] This basically prohibits Sun from engaging in any technical data communication relevant to a controlled item with CoCom-proscribed countries such as Russia without first obtaining explicit U.S. government approval.[22]

There is no specific criterion that establishes under what conditions controlled data must be pre-approved for export.[23] If an exporter knows in advance what type of information it plans to disseminate to organizations, individuals, or countries that require such licenses, then it can receive pre-approval from Commerce at that time on one overall license. The scope of a license can be very large, so that a great deal of information can be approved for export on one application, and such data could then be exported or transmitted on different occasions.[24]

On the other hand, if an exporter has not specifically listed on a previous license the technical data that it intends to export (such data as might commonly be generated by a joint-development, high-technology project where new information is constantly created), then it must seek a further license.[25] According to Sun, the complexity implicit in this process stifles the company's ability to conduct effective technical research with its Russian engineers. Sun must obtain a license for every letter or phone call that involves technical information if the controlled content of these is not specified on a pre-existing license.

In explaining why such rules are too cumbersome, Sun favors the analogy of two teams, one U.S. and one Russian, striving to develop a light bulb together. The Russian side provides a trial design. The U.S. side tests to see if it works. The U.S. side, however, cannot provide more feedback to the Russian team than "yes, the light bulb works" or "no, it doesn't work." To explain why "it doesn't work," the U.S. side needs to first gain problematic U.S. licensing approval, which can take several weeks to obtain.[26] Obviously, such restrictions impede joint development efforts in an industry where product obsolescence can occur within months.

Export Controls on Encryption Software

Finally, Sun's business in Russia has been complicated by U.S. government controls on the export of data encryption software to MCST. This software is used to secure business communications and the transmission of on-line proprietary data. Unless Sun can encrypt its communications, it is open to industrial espionage through eavesdropping by competitors or the Russian government. The United States will authorize the export of strong encryption products if these are only used between direct subsidiaries of U.S. firms. Similar licenses, however, are not generally approved for non-U.S. companies, as in the case between Sun and MCST (see Section V).

At first, Sun was only able to export a 40-bit key software encryption package. However, because this product was fairly weak, Sun considered using Russian encryption-ware instead. Although U.S. encryption products are strictly controlled for export to Russia, Russian encryption-ware can be imported to the United States. Sun then contacted the National Security Agency, explaining that the company would have to use a version of PGP obtained in Russia unless allowed to export its own encryption software (PGP is a 56-bit U.S. encryption software program originally loaded onto the Internet illegally). PGP is now widely available abroad, but is still illegal to export from the United States without a license. Based on this argument, the NSA recently agreed to sign off on Sun's use of its own UNIX DES 56-bit encryption kit for Sun's three MCST Russian sites. Sun may be the first U.S. company licensed to export DES-based encryption software to a Russian-owned company in Russia.[27]

The Impact of Export Controls

MCST is almost entirely geared toward research and development. There are no significant product sales to record. Thus, although license restrictions may reduce the productivity of Sun's effort, the absence of export controls would not guarantee a fruitful outcome. Sun can only measure the success of its Russian venture after products that are now being developed are brought to market, succeed in earning sales, and produce sufficient profit to ultimately recover sunk R&D investments. Moreover, though export controls have hindered or curtailed some activities, they have not stopped Sun from continuing to collaborate with its Russian partners.

Nevertheless, Sun is betting a portion of its resources and an intangible component of its future competitiveness (as measured in lost opportunity costs) on the long-range success of MCST.[28] Export controls have prevented Sun from making the most of this Russian talent and the export license process has set back Sun's schedule by over a year. Restrictions on technical discussions and use of encryption-ware have obstructed fluid communications between Sun's U.S. and Russian research engineers. The latter had to work without required equipment until computer controls were raised in March 1994. Finally, Sun must administer a complex export control compliance effort.

Conclusions

The Sun-MCST case is a clear example of the types of post-Cold War relationships that present difficult dilemmas for U.S. regulators and policymakers alike. Because U.S. technology could possibly find its way back into the Russian military, there is a certain gamble in allowing a joint-development, high-technology association between Sun and MCST.

On the other hand, the United States has an interest in providing Russian commercial firms with access to U.S. technology in order to expand the Russian economy and thus help foster democracy. Moreover, if U.S. firms are prevented from engaging in the Russian market, non-U.S. companies may step in. There is also the possibility that some of Sun's Russian talent could return to the Russian military-industrial complex. Likewise, MCST workers might even find employment in the defense or commercial efforts of other countries striving to acquire advanced technology.

Notes and References

Section I. Introduction

[1] The announcements were in September 1993, February 1994 and March 1994. For the September 1993 announcement see *Toward a National Export Strategy: Report to the U.S. Congress,* Trade Promotion Coordinating Committee, Ronald H. Brown, Chairman, (September 30, 1993). A fuller explanation is given by then Deputy Secretary of Defense William J. Perry in his press briefing on Computer Exports (October 15, 1993). See also, "BXA Issues New Regulations on Computer Decontrols & Lifting of the Embargo Against Vietnam," *The BXA Insider*, Vol. I, Issue 1, Department of Commerce, Washington, D.C. (April 1994); and T. Friedman, "U.S. Ending Curbs on High-Tech Gear to Cold War Foes," *The New York Times* (March 31, 1994). Congress is working to pass legislation reforming U.S. export controls and their administration; the previous law expired on 30 June 1994. See *The Export Administration Act of 1994: Administration Proposal* (February 24, 1994); and the current House and Senate versions of this legislation.

[2] "Fact Sheet: Nonproliferation and Export Control Policy," Office of the Press Secretary, The White House (September 27, 1993).

[3] See for example, G. Milhollin, "The Perils of Perry & Co.; Are They Soft on Nuclear Proliferation for the Sake of the Arms Industry," *The Washington Post* (February 6, 1994); and S. Bryen and M. Ledeen, "Decontrol Freaks; The Bush and Clinton Administrations' Unprecedented Giveaway of Secret Military Technology," *The American Spectator* (June 1994).

[4] For the best review of CoCom's history, see Michael Mastanduno, *Economic Containment: CoCom and the Politics of East-West Trade* (Ithaca, New York: Cornell University Press, 1992). This study provides historical background information on the U.S. export control system as well.

[5] There are other reasons why export controls to impede proliferation are unlikely to be as effective as the former CoCom controls: (1) not all potential suppliers of critical technologies participate in controlling their export, and those who do often have differing export criteria; (2) the development, for example, of indigenous capabilities for nuclear weapons manufacture is difficult to prevent because many of the associated technologies are 50-years old or older; and (3) the explosion in information resources, including the transfer of technical information across electronic networks, is very difficult to stop. See Mitchel B. Wallerstein, "Controlling Dual-Use Technologies in the New World Order," *Issues in Science and Technology* (Summer 1991), p. 75.

[6] See National Academy of Sciences, National Academy of Engineering, and Institute of Medicine, *Balancing the National Interest: U.S. National Security Export Controls and Global Economic Competition* (Washington, DC: National Academy Press, 1987).

[7] See *Global Trends in Computer Technology and Their Impact on Export Control*, National Research Council (Washington, D.C.: National Academy Press, 1988).

[8] See National Academy of Sciences, *Finding Common Ground: U.S. Export Controls in a Changed Global Environment* (Washington, DC: National Academy Press, 1991).

[9] See National Academy of Sciences, National Academy of Engineering, Institute of Medicine, and National Research Council, The *New Era in U.S. Export Controls: Report of a Workshop, September 24-25, 1991* (Washington, DC: National Academy Press, 1992).

[10] See U.S. Congress, Office of Technology Assessment, *Export Controls and Nonproliferation Policy,* (Washington, D.C.: U.S. Government Printing Office, May 1994).

[11] Other work has helped to focus our thinking about the relationship between export controls, national security, economic competitiveness, and development. See Gary K. Bertsch and Richard T. Cupitt, "Nonproliferation in the 1990s: Cooperation on Export Controls," *The Washington Quarterly* (Autumn 1993); Robert Kuttner "How 'National Security' Hurts National Competitiveness, "*Harvard Business Review* (Jan.-Feb 1991); Michael Mastanduno, "The United States Defiant: Export Controls in the Postwar Era" *Daedalus* (Fall, 1991); John H. Barton, "Conditionality and Development: The Technology Context," *Internationale Spectator* (November 1992); Harold Muller and Lewis A. Dunn, "Nuclear Export Controls and Supply Side Restraints: Options for Reform," (Published by the Mountbatten Center for International Studies, University of Southampton on behalf of the Programme for Promoting Nuclear Non-Proliferation, October 1993); Arvind Parkhe, "U.S. National Security Export Controls:

Implications for Global Competitiveness of U.S. High-Tech Firms," *Strategic Management Journal*,, Vol. 13 (1992); and Leonard S. Spector and Virginia Foran, "Preventing Weapons Proliferation: Should the Regimes be Combined?" (Stanley Foundation report of the 33rd Strategy for Peace, U.S. Foreign Policy Conference held October 22-24, 1992).

[12] See Cameron Binkley and John R. Harvey, *Export Controls on Dual-Use, High Technology: Implications for National/Economic Security: Summary of a Workshop held at Stanford University, October 18-19, 1993*, Center for International Security and Arms Control, (December 1993).

[13] The Commerce Control List (CCL) contains the various dual-use items whose export is controlled by the Commerce Department. It is found in the Export Administration Regulations (Part 799). The CCL is divided into ten broad technology categories, each of which is further divided into five product groups and assigned a specific export control classification number or ECCN. Thousands of items are individually controlled based on performance parameters and export destination.

[14] For a case study on machine tool export control costs, see *Export Controls and Nonproliferation,* U.S. OTA, op. cit., "Appendix A: Estimating the Economic Costs of Export Controls."

[15] J. David Richardson, *Sizing Up U.S. Export Disincentives* (Washington, D.C.: Institute for International Economics, 1993).

Section II. High-Technology Trade and Competition in International Markets

[1] For a comparison of the high-technology sectors included in the OECD International Standard Industrial Classification scheme and the U.S. Department of Commerce Standard Industrial Classification, see Laura D'Andrea Tyson, *Who's Bashing Whom: Trade Conflict in High-Technology Industries,* Institute for International Economics, 1992, pp. 20-21. For more detail, see T. A. Abbot, "Measuring High-Technology Trade: Contrasting International Trade Administration and Bureau of Census Methodologies and Results," *Journal of Economic and Social Measurement 17*; pp. 17-44, 1991.

[2] See Tyson, op. cit., pp. 32-33; based on data supplied by the National Science Foundation.

[3] See Tyson, op. cit., pp. 35-37; based on data from the US Department of Commerce, *Annual Survey of Manufactures,* 1989.

[4] See Tyson, op. cit., p. 38; based on data from the US Department of Labor, Bureau of Labor Statistics, "Employment and Earnings," March 1991.

[5] For a detailed study of the US textile industry see MIT Commission on Industrial Productivity, 1989, Study H, "The Textile Industry," pp. 288-302. See also Suzanne Berger et al., "The U.S. Textile Industry: Challenges and Opportunities in an Era of International Competition," *The Working Papers of the MIT Commission on Industrial Productivity,* 2 vols., Cambridge, MIT Press, 1989.

[6] Rebecca Smith and Thomas Farragher, "Why California Lost in Bid for Intel Plant," *San Jose Mercury News* (April 4, 1993), pp. 1, 24; Rebecca Smith, "Why Intel Jilted the Golden State," *San Jose Mercury News* (July 20, 1994), p. 1.

[7] See "Asia: Countries Sweeten Incentives for Foreign Investments," Inter Press Service (May 11, 1993). ASEAN includes the nations of Brunei, Indonesia, Malaysia, the Philippines, Singapore, and Thailand. In February 1995, Vietnam joined ASEAN's standing committee as an observer.

[8] For a detailed discussion of local spillover benefits from high-technology industries see Tyson, op. cit., 1992.

[9] See United Nations Center on Transnational Corporations, *World Investment Report 1991: The Triad in Foreign Direct Investment,* United Nations, New York, 1991; also see Julius, DeAnne, *Global Companies and Public Policy: The Growing Challenge of foreign Direct Investment,* Royal Institute of International Affairs, London, 1990.

[10] The development of global financial markets is encouraging additional FDI as sophisticated financial instruments are readily available to manage risk. Complex derivative financial instruments, such as currency options and swaps, are tools for firms interested in FDI projects and are used to manage the risk of currency fluctuations or market risks in foreign nations. These derivatives became possible as a result of the widespread application of information technologies to financial markets.

[11] Solow, Robert, "The Future of Employment in Advanced Societies," lecture delivered at The Conference on The Future of Industry in Advanced Societies, MIT Industrial Performance Center, September 8-9, 1993.

[12] Shimada, Haruo, "Synopsis of the Japan Commission on Industrial Performance Study," paper presented at the conference on The Future of Industry in Advanced Societies, MIT Industrial Performance Center, September 8-9, 1993.

[13] Political change, including the opening of Eastern Europe, the adoption of free market principles in the former Soviet Union and China, and the elimination of controls on travel and communications in many formerly repressive states also act to make it more difficult to maintain effective export controls.

[14] For an excellent discussion see Marvin B. Lieberman and David B. Montgomery, "First Mover Advantages," Stanford Graduate School of Business Research Paper No. 969 (October 1987).

[15] See National Research Council, *Global Trends in Computer Technology and Their Impact on Export Control,* (Washington, D.C.: National Academy Press, 1988).

[16] For one U.S. firm with 90% of its customers from the commercial sector, 80% of its product line was not on the market 12 months ago. In this environment, rapid market access and generation of volume sales (and increased market share) are essential for success. Export licensing delays can thus cause U.S. producers to lose their "first to market" advantage when facing, for instance, Taiwanese competitors.

[17] Those who argue that export controls are not a problem because a very large fraction of export licenses are eventually granted often do not consider that many sales are foregone because a firm never applies for a license at all because it is unwilling or unable to penetrate the "red tape" of the export control system. Roszel Thomsen of McKenny, Thomsen and Burke, private communication, April 29, 1994.

[18] Before Intel Corporation finally decided to build its new one billion dollar semiconductor fabrication plant in Rio Rancho, NM, it evaluated six sites, including sites in Singapore and Taiwan. Smith and Farragher, op. cit., pp. 1, 24.

[19] See J. David Richardson, *Sizing Up U.S. Export Disincentives* (Washington, D.C.: Institute for International Economics, 1993), pp. 14, 16 (Table 1.3), 132.

[20] Richardson's study found that the greatest economic impact of export controls involved trade with the former Soviet bloc; given recent developments and current economic conditions in many of these nations, the market size and trade level projected in his study may not be achieved for quite some time despite the relaxation of CoCom controls.

[21] Export controls can also be counterproductive to U.S. political and security interests if they are perceived as retarding economic development in the third world, or if they impede legitimate national undertakings. John Barton has pointed out that a "legitimacy crisis" could envelop an international control regime that seeks to control transfers of dual-use technologies to developing states who have not participated in the establishment of the regime. Under such conditions, the denial of technology with important commercial applications, for instance biotechnology and advanced computing, could breed contempt and non-cooperation on the part of some developing states. See John H. Barton, "Conditionality and Development: The Technology Context," *Internationale Spectator* (November 1992), p. 654.

Section III. National Security Implications of Export Controls on High-Performance Computing

[1] The Commerce Department characterizes computer capability in terms of Composite Theoretical Performance (CTP). The units are in Mtops (one million theoretical operations per second). In some but not all cases an Mtop is equivalent to the more recognizable unit, the Mflop (one million floating point operations per second). See "Technical Note: Composite Theoretical Performance (CTP)," Category 4 (Computers), Supplement No. 1 to Part 799.1 of the Commerce Control List. An account of the Commerce Department's adoption of the CTP metric for computers is found in D. Ames, D. Gibson, and B. Troy, "Composite Theoretical Performance," *Performance Evaluation Review* (August 1991).

[2] Calculations involved in nuclear warhead design include: (1) the hydrodynamic behavior of materials under strong shocks and high pressures, (2) neutron multiplication in supercritical plutonium, (3) boosting, (4) energy transport to the secondary, (5) compression and heating of the secondary and (6) thermonuclear burn. The speed at which a person could calculate by hand on an adding machine would be of the order of 1 flop—one floating point operation per second—or equivalently, 10^{-6} Mflops.

[3] For part of this discussion, we have drawn from an excellent report: Jack Worlton, "Some Myths About High Performance Computers and Their Role in the Design of Nuclear Weapons," Worlton & Associates Technical Report No. 32 (June 22, 1990).

[4] According to a Department of Commerce study completed in 1992, widespread foreign availability exists for computer workstations up to 67 Mtops. Some non-CoCom manufacturers can supply smaller numbers of computers up to 90 Mtops. More powerful systems, including those in excess of 195 Mtops (the previous Department of Commerce supercomputer threshold) will soon be available from suppliers such as Taiwan, if they are not already available. See *Foreign Availability Review of Computers—Executive Summary*, U.S. Department of Commerce, Bureau of Export Administration, Office of Foreign Availability, August 1992. See also, "Commerce Announces Positive Foreign Availability for Digital Computers," *U.S. Department of Commerce News*, Washington, D.C., (August 26, 1993).

[5] The Internet is an unclassified worldwide computer telecommunications network to which numerous companies, academic institutions and research organizations are connected. In principle, a foreign entity could, with the assistance of a "front" agency, purchase a supercomputer, keep it in the United States, and log on to it remotely over the Internet. This would be less straightforward than to use, for example, a mid-range Sun work station for nuclear weapons calculations. In the case of the complex, computer-intensive calculations required to design an

advanced stealth aircraft, or used in code breaking (both discussed subsequently in this section), these could conceivably be more difficult to hide from relevant authorities (or Internet hackers!). Also, for calculations requiring very high rates of input and output of data, computing over the Internet would be slow and ponderous.

[6] Nuclear warheads are designed to be one-point safe, that is, they will not produce significant nuclear yield in an accident if detonated at one point on the outer periphery of the high explosive. One-point safety calculations have received much attention lately at the weapons' labs. See J. Harvey and S. Michalowski, *Nuclear Weapons Safety and Trident: Issues and Options*, CISAC, Stanford University, August 1993. Other cases where enhanced calculational ability is useful include (1) modeling the complex Rayleigh-Taylor instabilities that enter in warhead design and that require very fine zoning in the region of interest, (2) enabling a better understanding of boost physics, and (3) modeling multipoint nuclear safety. In general, computers at the high-end of capability permit improved models that incorporate more of the physical processes of nuclear warhead operation, and enable better predictions of the results of nuclear tests. On the other hand, one analyst notes that "you don't need high-end computers to determine if the warhead will 'go bang.'" Private communication from Paul Brown and Robin Staffin, Lawrence Livermore National Laboratory, June 7, 1993.

[7] Other factors relate to why the U.S. nuclear design laboratories have traditionally purchased the most advanced supercomputers available: (1) the large budgets of the laboratories have permitted the purchase of these systems, (2) the heightened focus during the Cold War period on safety and reliability, and the extensive design trade-off studies deriving from the competitive nuclear design process in the United States, have justified the added expense of advanced computers, and (3) supercomputers can actually save money to the degree that they permit less reliance on costly nuclear tests of advanced weapons designs. These considerations are not generally relevant to the requirements of an emerging nuclear weapons state.

[8] A key concern, of course, are sales of advanced conventional weapons and technologies by industrial nations, including some U.S. allies, to potential enemies of the United States.

[9] Transcript of briefing with reporters, Dr. William Perry, Deputy Secretary of Defense, October 15, 1993.

[10] There are a number of tricks that can be used to help in this task. In one approach, the cryptanalyst is assumed to have secured the plaintext and encrypted forms of a single message, and the encryption algorithm; his job is to find the key by which the message was encoded so that other messages encoded with that key can be decoded. In this so-called "chosen-plaintext attack," the cryptanalyst compares the cleartext with the ciphertext to try to determine the key. Similarly, the cryptanalyst can look for known plaintext: a portion of a message that can be

deduced without decrypting it. For example, he may look for common eight-character ASCII groups such as " of the " (spaces before and after). Because this is an extremely common word grouping, it provides a doorway through which the cryptanalyst can try an attack.

[11] W. Diffie and M. Hellman, "Exhaustive Cryptanalysis of the NBS Data Encryption Standard," *Computer*, Vol. 10, No. 6 (June 1977), pp. 74-84. Also, M. Hellman, "A Cryptanalytic Time-Memory Trade Off," *IEEE Transactions on Information Theory*, IT-26 (1980) pp. 401-406, .

[12] See Michael J. Wiener, *Efficient DES Key Search*, Bell-Northern Research, Ottawa, Canada, unpublished manuscript, (August 20, 1993).

[13] See E. F. Brickell et al., *SKIPJACK Review: Interim Report: The SKIPJACK Algorithm*, report to the National Institute of Standards and Technology (NIST), (July 28, 1993). SKIPJACK is being proposed as the U.S. government standard to replace DES.

[14] E. F. Brickell et al., op. cit.

[15] There is still the "telnet" problem described earlier, although this may be mitigated somewhat in the case of high-end supercomputers.

Section IV. Export Controls on Microprocessors

[1] Microprocessors power computers ranging from simple business-oriented desktop systems to supercomputers designed to use many such devices in parallel. They are semiconductors that combine a range of complex electronic logic and arithmetic functions on a single integrated circuit platform or "chip." They are distinct from "memory" chips that are both less costly and easier to make.

[2] Since 1971, microprocessors have made tremendous increases in the computational power available and affordable to millions of personal, scientific and business users. High-speed microelectronic components are also key to enabling modern telecommunications. Together, the accelerated pace of change generated by widely distributed information technology has been identified by National Security Advisor Anthony Lake as one of the fundamental underlying trends of the post-Cold War era. See Anthony Lake, "From Containment to Enlargement," U.S. *Department of State Dispatch* (September 27, 1993), p. 659.

[3] Semiconductor Industry Association, *Annual Databook: Global and U.S. Semiconductor Competitive Trends, 1978-1991*, (San Jose, CA: Semiconductor Industry Association, 1992), p. 2.

[4] Semiconductor Industry Association, "Microelectronics: Vision for the 21st Century" (San Jose, CA: Semiconductor Industry Association, March 1994), pp. 3; 32.

[5] By advanced microprocessors, we mean those commercial models containing several million transistors per chip and able to process instructions with a word length of at least 32 data bits. These include the Intel 486 and Pentium chips, the PowerPC, and above.

[6] These figures from Dataquest are cited in, "Intel Increased Dominance in 1993 Microprocessor Market," *Business Wire* (February 18, 1994).

[7] William J. McClean, ed., *Status 1993: A Report of the Integrated Circuit Industry,* Integrated Circuit Engineering Corporation, pp. 6-30; Semiconductor Industry Association, *A New Calculus: Information Technology and Export Controls* (March 7, 1994), p. 6.

[8] Discussion with Mary O'Brien, Department of Commerce, Office of Export Enforcement (June 17, 1993).

[9] Ibid. (June 1, 17, 1993).

[10] R. S. Metcalfe, *The New Wizard War: How the Soviets Steal U.S. High Technology —And How We Give It Away* (Tempus Books of Microsoft Press: Redman Washington, 1988), pp. 130-134.

[11] Donovan Webster, "Chips Are a Thief's Best Friend," *The New York Times Magazine* (September 18, 1994), pp. 54-59.

[12] See "Intel in China High-tech Link-up," Reuter's Newswire (March 29, 1994). See also, Mark Clifford, "Hungary for Chips," *Far Eastern Economic Review* (September 10, 1992), pp. 60-61.

[13] Even under license, technology transfer helps broaden and deepen the technical skills and knowledge of foreign partners and contributes to the development of indigenous technological capabilities. Some critics argue that the export of U.S. production technology abroad helps create foreign competition.

[14] The manufacture of advanced microprocessors is a very complex and expensive endeavor. Even with government subsidies, most states simply do not have the technological or industrial capability necessary to make this economically fruitful, particularly given the current U.S. domination of the market.

[15] Imputed from data in William J. McClean, ed., op. cit., pp. 6-28. In addition to MOS-based microprocessors, the market includes microcontrollers and associated peripheral equipment. The United States held 59% of this market while Japan held 35%.

[16] David Kellar, "Taiwanese Vendor Develops Intel-Compatible 486SX, "Infoworld (October 18, 1993) p. 119; Alan Patterson, "Taiwan Cashing in on Chips," *Electronic Engineering Times* (January 1994), p. 4; Reuters, "UMC Aims

to Become World-class Chip Maker" (June 20, 1994). U.S. Department of Commerce, International Trade Administration, "Taiwan—Semiconductors" (December 27, 1993), (National Trade Data Bank market research report abridged from Shirley Wang, "The Semiconductor Market in Taiwan," American Institute, Taipei (June 1992)).

[17] In 1992, a U.S. government study called attention to the widespread global dissemination of advanced U.S. microprocessors, and the indigenous capabilities of several states to manufacture similar devices. The report concluded that it would not be feasible to reinstate past controls. See "GFW Eligible Semiconductor Devices," U.S. Department of Commerce, Bureau of Export Administration, Office of Foreign Availability (March 26, 1992) (unclassified executive summary).

[18] This is accomplished via the Export Administration Regulations (EAR) Supplement No. 1 to Section 799.1 (The Commodity Control List). The following Export Control Commodity Numbers (ECCNs) apply: 3A01A, 3A92F, 3A96G, and 3E01A.

[19] This is known as the "de minimis" rule. For a handful of states controlled for anti-terrorist reasons, the control threshold percentage drops to 10%.

[20] In 1991, the Commerce Department did consider the feasibility of curtailing eased restrictions on semiconductor controls. *Federal Register*, Vol. 56 (August 29, 1991), p. 42825.

[21] For example, if controls were reimposed on high-performance microprocessors, the delays in filling orders that could result from the licensing process might not significantly impact sales, because there are too few foreign suppliers available to fill the gap. On the other hand, foreign customers might settle for less sophisticated devices.

[22] Personal communication with David Rose, Intel Corp., (May 26, 1993).

[23] According to the National Academy of Sciences, few foreign firms not affiliated with U.S. subsidiaries regularly comply with U.S. re-export controls. In some cases neither do allied governments. For instance, in 1991 the Academy discovered that German companies "are advised [by their government] to comply only with the controls on re-exports of goods with 25 percent U.S.-origin parts or components." See National Academy of Sciences, National Academy of Engineering, and Institute of Medicine, *Balancing the National Interest: U.S. National Security Export Controls and Global Economic Competition* (Washington, DC: National Academy Press, 1987), p. 139; and National Academy of Sciences, *Finding Common Ground: U.S. Export Controls in a Changed Global Environment* (Washington, DC: National Academy Press, 1991), pp. 100-101.

[24] Although companies such as Acer in Taiwan have sought to adhere in the case of CoCom controls, most Taiwanese firms (and many of those in several other

newly industrialized states) freely sell to all buyers, including Russia and increasingly China. Taiwan has negotiated for accession to 5(k) status (a provision of the EAA), which refers to states who cooperate in export control matters with CoCom members. Full 5(k) status would mandate that Taiwan comply with U.S. re-export controls and establish as well an adequate system to regulate the export of its own products. At this time, Taiwan does not have full 5(k) status and is not obligated to exercise restraint over such exports. Taiwan's willingness to cooperate with the United States is at least partially motivated by recent U.S. reforms that have deregulated many items produced by Taiwan, such as semiconductors and computers, and by the realization that CoCom's successor is unlikely to be as strong an institution as CoCom in controlling exports. This cooperation should gain Taiwan greater access to the high-technology products of CoCom members.

[25] Until May 1994, the Commerce Department did not even measure the performance of microprocessors and computers with a comparable metric. This fact contributed to the disparity in the decontrol of each item relative to the other. The performance of computers is measured in Composite Theoretical Performance (CTP), which combines several factors including word length, number of floating point operations per second, and number of processors operating in parallel to arrive at a single unit of performance: millions of theoretical operations per second (Mtops). Microprocessors are evaluated according to different criteria, which includes databus width; the clock frequency of operation; the number of external links and data flow rates to other processors operating in parallel; and the instruction execution speed (measured in millions of instructions per second or MIPS). The Commerce Department has recently revised this last criteria so that the performance of both computers and microprocessors are now measured by the common CTP standard. See *Federal Register,* Vol. 59 (May 16, 1994) p. 25303. While more flexible than past standards, CTP is itself unwieldy and not used outside export control circles.

[26] Industry sources claim that advanced microprocessors now in development will have performances ranging from 750 to 1000 Mtops. For exports to civilian end-users in states of the former Soviet Union, the current threshold for control is 1000 Mtops. As recently as December 1993, the threshold level above which computer exports to Russia were controlled was 12.5 Mtops.

[27] See S1496, "The High Technology Indexation Act of 1993," introduced by Senator Feinstein (D-CA).

Section V. Export Controls on Mass-Market Software With Encryption

[1] Encryption is the science of encoding messages so that, without extraordinary effort, only those with the proper key can decipher them. For details see "Answers to Frequently Asked Questions About Today's Cryptography," RSA Laboratories,

Revision 2.0, October 1993. Mass-market software is software that is generally available to the public by being (1) sold from stock at retail selling points without restriction, and (2) designed for installation by the user without substantial support from suppliers.

[2] The National Security Agency (NSA) has responsibility for protecting U.S. government and military communications, and for intercepting and reading overseas message traffic relevant to U.S. national security. NSA has pressed for continued export controls on encryption devices. Beyond these roles the NSA, by law, also provides code-breaking support to the FBI and advises the National Institute of Standards and Technology (NIST) regarding domestic communications and data security products and standards.

[3] In one Defense Department test, the source code for DES, an export-restricted encryption scheme, was located and retrieved in about three minutes over the Internet. See John Perry Barlow, "A Plain Text on Crypto Policy," *Microtimes* (November 15, 1993), p. 222.

[4] Giggi Bisson, "Global Software Expansion is Hampered by Strict U.S. Laws," *MacWEEK* (June 14, 1993), p. 39.

[5] These algorithms are 40-bit versions of RSA Inc.'s RC-2 and RC-4 encryption systems. They are relatively weak and supposedly can be rapidly broken by NSA. Encryption systems such as DES (56-bit key) and Skipjack (80-bit key), used in the Clipper chip, are often characterized as "strong" systems. One possible reason for the seven-day wait is to provide NSA an opportunity to keep track of which customers are purchasing what encryption products. See Jonathan Groner, "When It Comes to Software, U.S. Sees Military Hardware; Concern Over Spread of Encryption Codes Hurts Exports," *The Connecticut Law Tribune* (December 21, 1992): p. 12; and *Federal Register* Vol. 57 (July 20, 1992) p. 32148).

[6] H.R. 3627, introduced by Reps. Cantwell and Manzullo, November 22, 1993, to amend the Export Administration Act of 1979 with respect to the control of computers, related equipment, and software (including for data encryption).

[7] See Export *Controls: Issues in Removing Militarily Sensitive Items From the Munitions List,* U.S. Government Accounting Office, GAO/NSIAD-93-97, Washington, D.C., (March 1993), pp. 11-12; 21-23.

[8] Such transfers can occur under State licenses as well, given the difficulties inherent in re-export controls.

[9] See letter from Vice President Gore to Rep. Cantwell, July 20, 1994; and "Gore Shifts Stance on Chip Code," *New York Times* (July 21, 1994), p. 1; and "EFF Analysis of Vice President Gore's Letter on Cryptography Policy," Electronic Freedom Foundation, July 22, 1994. In a key-escrow system, such as the U.S. government's Clipper initiative for telephonic communications, two unique keys

are necessary to decode messages encrypted by a Clipper chip. For a particular chip, the two keys would be held "in escrow" separately in two government databases. The keys would be released only to officials with legal authorization to conduct a wiretap. See "Statement by the Press Secretary," The White House, Washington, D.C., April 16, 1993.

[10] See U.S. Congress, House of Representatives, "Omnibus Export Administration Act of 1994," 103rd Congress, 2d Session, House Report No. 103-531, Parts I, II, III, and IV, and H.R. 4663, June 28, 1994, Section 117(c) (1)-(3). This legislation (and similar Senate legislation) was pending as the 103rd Congress came to a close.

[11] See Public Law 103-160, "National Defense Authorization Act for Fiscal Year 1994," Section 267, November 30, 1993. See also, "A Study of National Cryptography Policy," National Research Council, Washington, D.C., September 14, 1994.

[12] Adm. John M. McConnell, Director, National Security Agency, testimony before the Subcommittee on Technology and Law of the Committee of the Judiciary, U.S. Senate (May 3, 1994), p. 6.

[13] Louis J. Freeh, Director of the FBI, testimony before the Subcommittee on Technology and the Law of the Committee on the Judiciary, U.S. Senate and the Subcommittee on Civil and Constitutional Rights of the Committee on the Judiciary, U.S. House of Representatives (March 18, 1994), p. 5.

[14] Ibid., pp. 17-18.

[15] It is generally believed that NSA computers are programmed to do "key word" searches on global communications to identify traffic relevant to U.S. security. For example, computers may monitor traffic in the Middle East and call to the attention of analysts any message in which the word "maraging" (a type of steel used in the fabrication of rotors for uranium-enrichment centrifuges) is mentioned.

[16] This view of NSA's concerns is held, among others, by Martin Hellman. See Mary Eisenhart, "Encryption, Privacy & Data Security," *Microtimes* (March 8, 1993), p. 118. The use of strong encryption is, in itself, not sufficient to prevent the NSA, or a determined foreign intelligence service, from collecting and decoding specific messages. With sophisticated computers even strong encryption algorithms can eventually be broken. Still, encryption will make it more difficult and costly to do this, and will limit significantly the volume of traffic that can be exploited within reasonable periods. Due to the limited throughput, intelligence organizations will need to make difficult choices concerning which traffic is, or is not, to be decrypted.

[17] For example, the fact that a strong encryption algorithm in software can be rapidly downloaded from the Internet and exploited in telecommunications, does not mean that the average user will do this in order to protect the privacy of his or her own messages. In a "seamless" system, encryption and decryption operations are transparent to the user.

[18] See Justin Fielding, "What Is This Thing Called Lotus Notes?", *PC World* (February 1994), p. L12. In a public-key system each user has a public and private key, which are related. The message sender first queries a database to find the public key of the recipient and then encrypts the message with it. The message is transmitted and then decrypted with the private key of the intended recipient. The public-key system has the benefit that it does not require secure key exchange. Public and private keys are generated using a "one-way" mathematical function having the feature that it is easy to encrypt a message with the recipient's public key, but impractical to decipher the message without access to the private key.

[19] Doug Van Kirk, "Data Encryption Facilitates Confidentiality: Security Requirements Are Increasing as Corporate LANs Carry More Strategic Data," *Infoworld* (March 22, 1993), p. 62.

[20] M. Ratcliffe, "ASDSP Encryption Protects Network Sessions," *MacWEEK* (July 12, 1993), pp. 45-47.

[21] Common Channel Signaling is a telecommunications technique that separates a message's source and destination addresses from the message content. The two separate pieces are time stamped so that they can be joined later, and then sent along two different communications paths to the destination switch. This separation reduces the efficacy of traffic analysis and eavesdropping by making it more difficult to target particular source and destination addresses. Telecommunications routed over a fiberoptic link are very difficult to intercept without tapping directly into the line.

[22] This view is held by Whitfield Diffie, Sun Microsystems, private communication, April 18, 1994.

[23] Estimates of "lost sales" associated with current export controls range from a few tens of millions to $9 billion per year—a very large range of uncertainty. For example, the Business Software Alliance (BSA) claims that software exporters lose between $6 to 9 billion per year. This widely cited figure is based on a BSA-contracted survey of Fortune 500 companies in the United States. In this survey, a third of the companies responding indicated a willingness to purchase foreign-manufactured, mass-market software products incorporating encryption if U.S. products were unavailable. The BSA then multiplied the total revenue to U.S. firms from sales of such products (estimated between $17 to 27 billion for 1991) by one-third to deduce the $6-9 billion range. This approach is dubious for a number of reasons. First, no information is provided on the fraction of total revenue deriving

from purchases of these products by corporate respondents to the BSA survey. Second, the total revenue figures cited include all sales, both domestic and foreign; losses due to export restrictions, of course, only affect the second figure. In this regard, the loss range estimate should be reduced by a factor of two because, according to SPA's estimate, overseas sales account for about 40% of total revenue. Indeed, the revenue lost as a result of foreign firms not being able to buy U.S. encryption software products could be large. See "U.S. Software Industry Urges Further Liberalization of Export Controls to Include Mass-Marketed Software with Encryption Capabilities," Business Software Alliance, Washington, D.C., 6 October 1993. Jim Bidzos of RSA Inc., a data security firm, disputes the BSA claim that U.S. software firms are losing billions of dollars from export controls, although he argues that there is a real threat that a market of several tens of millions of dollars may be lost. Jim Bidzos, RSA Inc., private communication, May 12, 1994.

[24] Jim Bidzos, RSA Inc., private communication, May 12, 1994. At least one U.S. producer of encryption software products, Trusted Information Systems (TIS), started a British subsidiary in 1992 to reproduce its product line "from scratch" overseas, thus avoiding U.S. export controls. This was legal so long as the TIS parent firm did not transfer to its UK subsidiary relevant U.S. technology. Because TIS's U.S. programmers could have no part in the subsidiary's activities, it hired British programmers. Thus, compliance with U.S. law caused TIS to create jobs for foreign workers. Products produced in the UK, of course, would be subject to that country's export controls. See Testimony by Stephen T. Walker, Trusted Information Systems, Inc. to the Subcommittee on Economic Policy, Trade and Environment, Committee on Foreign Affairs, U.S. House of Representatives (October 12, 1993), pp. 14-15; and James Aley, "How Not to Help High Tech," *Fortune* , 16 May 1994, p. 100.

[25] The SPA began a study of foreign availability in 1993 and has identified more than 200 foreign producers of stand-alone encryption products. See Stephen T. Walker, President, Trusted Information Systems, Inc., testimony before the Subcommittee on Technology and the Law, Committee on the Judiciary, U.S. Senate, May 3, 1994), p. 15 and attachment. See also Lance Hoffman, "SPA Study of Foreign Availability of Cryptography," *SPA News,* March 1994, pp. U1-U4.

[26] Sun Microsystems assesses its total administrative costs for export control compliance at approximately $1 million per year. Interview with Hans Leumers, Sun Microsystems, March 12, 1993.

[27] Luke Alexander and Hans Leumers, Sun Microsystems, private communication, February 15, 1994.

[28] Companies are typically more concerned about spying by competitors than by foreign governments, although it is not unknown for intelligence organizations to supply domestic firms with proprietary information garnered from the foreign competition. Those who might suggest that the relatively weak encryption schemes

currently available for export are sufficient to protect corporate communications may not have factored in this latter point. See Roderick P. Deighen, "Welcome to the Cold War II; Industrial Espionage," *Chief Executive (U.S.)*, No. 82 (January 1993), p. 42.

[29] See Michael Alexander, "Industrial Espionage with U.S. Runs Rampant," *Computerworld* (March 4, 1991), p. 64. In one startling case, an MCI employee, who tapped one of the company's long-distance telephone switches, stole 60,000 credit card numbers and was responsible for $50 million in fraudulent charges as a result of reselling the numbers to computer hackers. See Bill Gertz, "Electronic Crime Threatens 'Integrity of the Long-distance Phone System,'" *Washington Times* , October 24, 1994, p. 3.

[30] See Loi numero 90-1170 parue au Journal Officiel du 30 Decembre 1990 (Art. 28). The degree to which such rules can be enforced is subject to debate.

[31] See Export of Goods (Control) Order 1994 (SI 1994 No 1191) (April 24, 1994), Sch 1, Part III Group 3 Industrial Goods: Category 5 Telecommunications and Information Security.

[32] Britain's Ministry of Trade and Industry, which is responsible for export licensing, has made some exceptions. Cellular systems using the A5 algorithm have been authorized for Australia, Hong Kong, New Zealand, Qatar, Singapore, and the United Arab Emirates. See "Taiwanese Operator Complains of Second-Class GSM Citizenship," *FinTech Mobile Communications* (July 28, 1994).

[33] See "Germany: Problems With Public Encryption," *Intelligence Newsletter* (February 24, 1994). Also, private communication (via email) from W. H. Sonnemans, April 20, 1994, concerning the proposed Dutch policies on encryption.

[34] See Joshua Greenbaum, "The Clipper Chip in Europe," *Open Computing* (formerly *UnixWorld*), (August 1994), p. 37; and "U.S. Vendor Pushes International Clipper Chip Scheme," *Computer Fraud & Security Bulletin* (June 1994).

[35] Clint Brooks, Scott Charney, et al, "Crypto Policy Perspectives," *Communications of the ACM* (August 1994).

[36] Because encryption software is classified as a munition by the State Department, U.S. companies cannot, as they can for most items controlled by the Commerce Department, apply for relief based on the argument that widespread "foreign availability" of a product undermines the effectiveness of controls on that product. Items on the Munitions List are unlikely to be sold to potential adversaries even if comparable goods are available elsewhere.

Section VI. The Nature of U.S. Unilateral Controls and Their Implications

[1] The United States also maintains unilateral export controls on certain products or destinations for reasons of short supply and nuclear non-proliferation. Short supply controls apply mainly to petroleum and lumber exports. Nuclear-related items require licensing as mandated under section 309 (c) of the Nuclear Non-Proliferation Act of 1978 (as amended) and are typically denied for export to states of proliferation concern.

[2] Export Administration Act of 1979, Section 3 (2) (B), as amended in 1981, 1985, and 1988.

[3] Neither Cuba nor North Korea are currently deemed active sponsors, but remain officially sanctioned due to their past behavior, current status as safe havens (in the case of Cuba,) and potential to engage in large-scale terrorist activity on short notice (in the case of North Korea). See Patrick N. Theros, "Trends in Global Terrorism," *Department of State Dispatch* , June 20, 1994. Pakistan has recently been under consideration for its support of violent separatist activity in Kashmir.

[4] Only general license items (those not requiring an individual validated license) can be exported to Iran. This was mandated in the National Defense Authorization Act signed into law in October 1992.

[5] In the Boeing 737 the ring laser gyro for the inertial navigation system is the only component subject to control. It is considered a munitions item and is controlled by the State Department. Engineering design and manufacturing processes related to aircraft and engine advanced composite materials, and "hot section" components for certain engines are technologies subject to control. Private communication, Kent McCormick, The Boeing Company, October 1993.

[6] "News Breaks," *Aviation Week and Space Technology* (September 28, 1992), p. 28; "Boeing Asks to Sell Jets to Iran Air," The *New York Times,* (September 30, 1992), p. D5.

[7] As a result of the embargo, in August 1993 Iran Air notified Boeing that it was terminating negotiations for the purchase of the 737 aircraft.

[8] Iran is a fairly large market for several U.S. allies, but not for the United States. According to the IMF, in 1992 Germany and Japan exported goods to Iran worth $5.6 billion and $2.9 billion, respectively, compared to $0.8 billion worth of mostly humanitarian goods from the United States. See *Direction of Trade Statistics Yearbook* (Washington, D.C.: International Monetary Fund, 1993), p. 226 (Iran). Richardson estimates that U.S. firms sustain, on average, a $1.5 billion annual export shortfall as a result of the Iran embargo. See J. David Richardson, *Sizing Up*

U.S. Export Disincentives, Institute for International Economics, Washington, DC (1993) pp. 97-98, 104. Both Bush and Clinton initiated as yet unsuccessful diplomatic efforts to curb U.S. allies' trade with Iran, including in military-related items. "German Exports Helping Iran Rearm," *The Washington Post* (December 6, 1992), p. 33; and "Japan Reluctant to Back Embargo on Iran," *The Washington Post* , (November 14, 1992), p. 21.

[9] The foreign (mostly U.S.) content in Airbus aircraft is: A310-300: 30%, A320: 17% (with substantial U.S. content in the jet engines), A330-300: 30% (with U.S. engines), 10% (with Rolls Royce engines), A330-600: 29%, and A340-300: 22%. See "Responses of Airbus Industrie and Airbus Industrie of North America to Questions Asked at Hearing on April 15, 1993 (Before the U.S. International Trade Commission)," Renee Martin-Nagle, Corporate Counsel, Airbus Industrie of North America, Inc., p. 2; cited in *Global Competitiveness of U.S. Advanced-Technology Manufacturing Industries: Large Civil Aircraft,* U.S. International Trade Commission, Washington, D.C., Publication 2667 (August 1993), p. 4-12.

[10] In the Bush administration, the United States granted Airbus permission, on a one-time basis, to sell two (possibly three) A300-600 aircraft to Iran Air. These aircraft use GE CF-60 engines and exceed the 10% criterion for U.S. content. Two were scheduled for delivery in 1994. One U.S. industry official speculated that Iran may consider buying the A330 (with Rolls Royce engines) in order to circumvent U.S. re-export controls. See "Iran Air: Carrier to Buy Airbus Planes with Engines Made by GE," *Wall Street Journal* (April 28, 1992), p. A16; and S. Auerbach and R. M. Weintraub, "U.S. Aircraft Makers Press for Permission to Sell Jets to Iran," *Washington Post* (April 9, 1993), pp. F1-F2. More recently, see "M. S. Lelyveld, "Questions Fly Over Sale of GE Engines to Iran," *Journal of Commerce,* (January 20, 1995), p. 1.

[11] Boeing is not the only U.S. company to have this problem. In early 1993, Sundstrand, a U.S. aerospace firm, received an order from a European firm that manufactures small commuter aircraft for the purchase of several GPS navigation units built by Data Control, then a subsidiary of Sundstrand. These units were to be used in eight aircraft that were to be sold to the government of Iran for civilian use in aerial mapping. Sundstrand sought a license from the Commerce Department to sell the navigation units to the European company because company officials were aware that the aircraft were to be exported to Iran. The license was rejected. Officials of the European company were furious about the denial, claiming that their business was jeopardized. They threatened not only to seek out European suppliers of these units but to cease future business with Sundstrand on other deals unrelated to Iran. Sundstrand went back to Commerce, which again rejected the license. Although Sundstrand eventually retained its business with the European company, relations between the two firms were affected. Interview with Dick Johann and Brad Considine, Sundstrand Corporation, August 8, 1994. Sundstrand was probably not obligated to seek an individual license for the sale; rather it was the European firm's obligation to seek re-export authorization if the

value of U.S. content in the aircraft exceeded ten percent, which apparently was not the case.

[12] Iranian commercial airliners could be used to transport weapons or terrorists to areas of conflict. Also, with extensive and costly modifications, they could perhaps be converted into a weapons delivery vehicle. But such arguments do not carry much weight. Iran already has a reasonably sophisticated air force and, in most cases, would not need to use commercial airliners for military purposes. Indeed, the Russians may be selling Backfire bombers to Iran, which have weapons delivery capabilities well beyond those of a modified 737.

[13] EPCI was implemented at the end of 1990 in response to President Bush's desire to take stronger measures to restrain proliferation. Among other things, he expanded the obligations of U.S. firms with regard to export controls and export administration. See Executive Order 12735, "Chemical and Biological Weapons Proliferation," November 16, 1990, and "Fact Sheet on the Enhanced Proliferation Control Initiative," The White House, Washington, D.C., December 13, 1990.

[14] To date, no U.S. company has been prosecuted for an EPCI violation. Corporate officials take EPCI seriously, however, because of their potential liability and the desire to avoid negative publicity. There is some concern, expressed by large exporters, that very small exporters could afford to ignore EPCI rules, knowing that there is little actual likelihood of criminal prosecution and that the damage from any negative press coverage would be less threatening to a small business.

[15] In one such case, Varian, a high-technology manufacturer of medical and scientific instruments, sought in April 1993 an advisory opinion from the Commerce Department concerning whether it would be permitted, under EPCI, to export equipment (otherwise subject to only a general [G-Dest] license) to four previous customers in Iran. Specifically, Varian wanted clarification under the EPCI "know" standard prior to conducting further business with them. On April 19, 1993, Commerce replied regarding three of the cases but declined to respond to the fourth. More than a year later in June 1994, Varian received a "request-for-bid" offer from this fourth entity. When Varian contacted Commerce to check on the status of the advisory opinion, it was told that "the case was still pending review." Varian has had similar delays in other cases. Private communication from Carol Henton, Varian (September 18, 1994). See also "EPCI is Broken—Here is How" (Letter to the Editor), *Export Control News* (July 31, 1994), p. 11.

[16] See "Guidance; Validated License Requirements Based on Missile or Chemical and Biological (CBW) Weapons End-Uses; Activities of U.S. Persons," *Federal Register,* Vol. 58 (December 23, 1993), p. 68029.

[17] See H. Muller, et. al., "From Black Sheep to White Angel? The New German Export Control Policy," Peace Research Institute Frankfurt, PRIF Reports No. 32, (January 1994). See also, Thomas Lucey, "Rule Shift May Aid German Firms;

Changes in Export Restrictions Would Open More Markets," *Defense News* (December 19, 1994), p. 18.

[18] See "EU: Control of Dual-Use Goods Exports is a Step towards a Joint Control System," *Reuter Textline Agence Europe* (December 28, 1994). The "has been informed" language implies several possible mechanisms for implementation: (1) a list of proscribed destinations could be provided to exporters, (2) companies could seek an advisory opinion from authorities on certain sales of potential concern, or (3) export control authorities could be notified of all impending sales, for example, by a prenotification requirement (if not an export license application), and could move to block sales of concern within a fixed period of time. In any case, the EU catch-all rule seems to steer away from imposing an explicit obligation on firms to "know" their customers; rather, the burden seems to be on the EU authorities to "inform." For further details, see "Section: Completing the Internal Market; Control of Goods; Dual-Use Goods and Technologies," Commission of the European Communities INFO-92, January 17, 1995.

[19] U.S. Congress, Office of Technology Assessment, *Export Controls and Nonproliferation Policy,* (Washington, D.C.: U.S. Government Printing Office, May 1994), pp. 8-9, 38-39, 59-63.

[20] For the MTCR sanctions law, see Defense Authorization Act, P.L. 101-510, 101st Congress, 2nd session, 104 STAT 1738-50, November 1990. This law amends Section 6 of the EAA (50 U.S.C. App. Section 2405), adds a new Section 11B to the EAA (50 U.S.C. App. 2410(a)) and adds a new Chapter 6 to the AECA (22 U.S.C. Section 2795(b)). To date, the United States has imposed MTCR sanctions against entities in Russia, India, Pakistan, and China, as well as in Iran, North Korea, South Africa, and Syria. Sanctions were required against one unidentified entity (possibly in Israel) but rescinded for reasons of national security.

[21] Sanctions were also imposed in June 1991, but later lifted when China agreed to adhere to the MTCR.

[22] H. Sokolski, "U.S. Satellites to China," *International Defense Review,* No. 4, 1994.

[23] See "The U.S. and China: Curbing Missile and Nuclear Proliferation; Secretary Christopher, Chinese Vice Premier and Foreign Minister Qian, Joint Statements," *U.S. Department of State Dispatch,* Vol. 5, No. 42, October 17, 1994. Also, D. Williams, "U.S. Deal with China Allows High-Tech Sales in Exchange for Pledge, *The Washington Post* (October 5, 1994), p. 6.

[24] *The Export Administration Act of 1994: Administration Proposal,* Section 12A, February 24, 1994.

[25] These discretionary sanctions would be imposed in proportion to the harm the sanctioned behavior caused to U.S. national security and non-proliferation

interests, and could include one or more of the following: termination of foreign aid and arms sales, denial of credit and loans, further export restrictions, import restrictions, downgrading or suspending of diplomatic relations, and revocation of landing rights for foreign air carriers.

Appendix I. The U.S. Export Control System Simplified

[1] BXA has four major divisions: the Office of Export Licensing (OEL), the Office of Export Enforcement (OEE), the Office of Technology and Policy Analysis (OTPA), and the Office of Foreign Availability (OFA). The OFA is important for exporters as it determines the merits of dropping controls for items that are freely available from overseas sources. Commerce is currently reorganizing these offices.

[2] The Export Administration Act (EAA) must be re-authorized every three years and its latest version is currently pending before Congress. Since 1979, Congress has amended the Act three times, most importantly in 1985 and 1988. The EAA expired in 1990 due to a presidential veto, but has been extended until now through executive order under provisions of the International Emergency Economic Powers Act. The first EAA was enacted into law in 1949.

[3] Codified under Chapter VII of volume 15 of the U.S. Code of Federal Regulations, and issued on an annual basis as a separate publication by the Department of Commerce.

[4] Export Administration Regulations, (EAR) Supplement No. 1 to Section 799.1, Commerce Control List [CCL]. The CCL incorporates CoCom's Core List, dual-use nuclear-related items not under NRC control (required by the NNPA), Category 2 items of the MTCR Annex, items related to chemical or biological weapons proliferation, and lists countries to which items are controlled for anti-terrorist, crime control, or other foreign policy purposes.

[5] There are several other special general licenses, including for exports of technology or technical data.

[6] EAR Section 771.23(b) defines countries eligible for GFW status. Most are non-communist or were never a member of the Communist Bloc. Exclusions are also made for Iran and Syria, among others.

Appendix II. The Implications of the Microprocessor for Supercomputing

[1] See F. Baskett and J. L. Hennessy, "Microprocessors: From Desktops to Supercomputers," *Science* (August 13, 1993), for a discussion of how advanced

microprocessors have begun to mimic the functions of supercomputers and how they are likely soon to surpass supercomputer performance capabilities.

[2] With the future portending widespread access to ever increasing computational power, a premium may well be placed on the efficient design and use of software, as the U.S. military realizes. For instance, the latest F-16D fighters employ 15 computers requiring 236,000 lines of code. The Air Force expects six million lines of code to be required for the next generation F-22 fighter. According to one estimate, software programmers write an average of 10 lines of code per day, which means that dramatic improvements in the way software is written and integrated into various systems will become more important in the future. See John Rhea, "Software in Tug-of-War, Custom vs. Off-the-Shelf: Budgetary Constraints Require Increasing Sophistication from a Few, Selected Systems," *National Defense* (December 1993), pp. 36-37.

[3] The CPU is the main computational element of the computer, constructed using microelectronic technology. It can be assembled as a device whose principal components are fully integrated onto a single self-contained chip (typical of microprocessors). Alternatively, the functions of a much larger and more able device can be divided across numerous separate chips.

[4] Even the simplest MPP systems using off-the-shelf microprocessors still rely on some customized hardware, technology, or software (especially source code). This is where control efforts must focus. See S. E. Goodman and P. Wolcott, "High-Performance Computing: Controllability and Cooperation," (A Discussion Paper prepared for the Russian-American Workshop on Dual-Use Technologies and Conversion, National Research Council and the Russian Academy of Sciences, Moscow, December 13-19, 1992).

[5] Cutbacks in government research funding and procurement are other reasons. Agencies that would once have needed supercomputer access are also finding it more cost-effective to use individual or clustered workstations instead. See John Markoff, "In Supercomputers, Bigger and Faster Means Trouble," *New York Times* (August 7, 1994), pg. F5.

[6] The Param computer, as it is known, is reportedly able to perform 6 billion floating point operations per second. C.T. Mahabharat, "India Producing Own Supercomputer," *Newsbytes* (April 8, 1992). Although this case is used as an example of how export controls foster indigenous development, the system's own designers seemed to consider the Param more as an interim step in parallel system development, than as a commercial system. No one, so far, appears to have actually purchased one, although some may have been "exported" as gifts. Dr. Arogyaswami Paulraj, formerly of the Center for the Development of Advanced Computing (CDAC), India (interviewed at Stanford University, April 18, 1993.)

[7] Reuters, "NTT Ties up with Silicon Graphics in Multimedia" (June 8, 1994); The Associated Press, "AT&T, Silicon Form Venture" (June 22, 1994).

[8] Jean S. Bozman, "SGI Expands 'Low-cost' Supercomputer Line" *Computerworld* (July 4, 1994), p. 24. David Evans, "Silicon Launches Bargain Basement Supercomputers" *Computer Weekly* (February 4, 1993), p. 10.

[9] Multiprocessor and MPP-type computers may not fully replace traditional supercomputers. As in the mainframe market, supercomputer producers now have a relatively large installed hardware and software base that will make switching costs hard to ignore. Some problems may also not be soluble by current techniques used in MPP computing.

Appendix III. Export Controls and Sun Microsystems in Russia

[1] "The Top 50 U.S. Industrial Exporters," *Fortune* (August 22, 1994). p. 132.

[2] Sun's second project involved a Russian enterprise known as Elvis+ (Electronic Computer and Information Systems). The Sun-Elvis+ project, which was recently completed, was also affected by export controls.

[3] Sun's operations are also negatively affected by the country's unstable business environment and uncooperative government bureaucracy.

[4] Shawn P. McCarthy, "High-tech Partnerships between U.S. and Russian Groups Still Clouded by Concerns over Our National Security, "Government *Computer News* (June 7, 1993) p. 50.

[5] At ITMVT, Babaian developed the Elbrus I and Elbrus II multiprocessing supercomputers, whose major uses include space missions, nuclear power plants, weapons design, and the operation of anti-ballistic missile defense systems. Peter Wolcott, *Soviet Advanced Technology: The Case of High-Performance Computing*, unpublished dissertation (Arizona: University of Arizona, 1993), p. 131. Most sales were to the military-industrial complex. The Elbrus III prototype was slated to be somewhat comparable to the Cray Y-MP C90. State orders for the Elbrus III have dried up and Babaian has had great difficulty obtaining state funds to finish the project.

[6] Wolcott, p. 187. Including multiprocessor-based systems compatible with Sun's SPARC station and Solaris computers. Other efforts include upgrading various compilers, writing various debugging, testing, and maintenance programs, and developing a UNIX-based operating system.

[7] Mark Hall and John Barry, *Sunburst, The Ascent of Sun Microsystems* (Chicago: Contemporary Books, 1990), p. 162.

[8] Supercomputer processors and microprocessors share some common technical characteristics. For example, the processors developed by Babaian for his Elbrus machines use a reduced instruction set architecture that facilitates technology sharing with Sun and is one of the reasons for Sun's interest in MCST. Beyond financial interests, Babaian has wanted to acquire Sun's SPARC instruction set to use in combination with Elbrus III techniques in order to design a more advanced, SPARC-compatible "Elbrus IV" system. Wolcott, p. 187; Ron Wilson and Nicolas Mokhoff, "Sun and Russians: Phase 2," *Electronic Engineering Times* (September 7, 1992), p. 18.

[9] These are the accounts given by both Sun and Babaian. See Arthur Fisher, "Computer Czar," *Popular Science* (August 1994). Top Russian designers are able to help optimize and even write microelectronic software for advanced Western microprocessors of the type Sun is developing. However, it is generally understood by Western experts on Soviet/Russian computer technology that the Russian semiconductor manufacturing industry is not able to produce advanced microprocessors. Daniel L. Burghart, in *Red Microchip: Technology Transfer, Export Control, and Economic Restructuring in the Soviet Union* (Aldershot, England: Dartmouth Publishing Co., 1992), gives a good account of why the Soviet/Russian computer industry fell so far behind the West.

[10] Reliable large-scale Soviet/Russian semiconductor manufacturing peaked at the 1.5 micron range or 30,000 transistors per chip. Wolcott, p. 505. By comparison, an Intel Pentium microprocessor contains over 3 million transistors with feature sizes in the .6 micron range.

[11] CISAC interview with Malcolm Wing and Luke Alexander, Sun Microsystems (January 26, 1994).

[12] The U.S. firm Auriga estimates that labor costs for U.S. programmers is $35 to $50 per hour *plus* overhead and benefits whereas Russian programmers only account for $7 to $10 per hour *including* overhead and benefits. Auriga has hired a group of Russian programmers to work for it in Moscow. McCarthy, p. 50.

[13] Information from Sun's export license, U.S. Department of Commerce, Bureau of Export Administration, Export License D167333 (April 27, 1993), Section 1(c) (Conditions of Approval). Controlled items are listed on the Commerce Control List (CCL) according to their coded export commodity Export Control Classification Number (ECCN). Those specifically relating to Sun's MCST license are ECCNs 3E01A, 4E01A, 4E02A, 4D01A, 4D02A, and 4D03A. See EAR Supplement No. 1 to Section 799.1 (The Commodity Control List).

[14] "U.S. Ending Curbs on High-Tech Gear to Cold War Foes," *New York Times* (March 31, 1994).

[15] Tom R. Halfhill, "Sun Expands Alliance With Russian Computer Scientists," *Microbytes* (November, 1992), p. 32. At the time, the Russians could not buy the software they had helped to develop.

[16] Advanced computers are necessary to design advanced microprocessors. By freeing up controls on high performance computers, Sun was able to accelerate MCST's processor development schedule. Personal communication with Carolyn Turbyfill, Sun Microsystems (April 5, 1994).

[17] Statement by Tim Dwyer and John Gage, Sun Microsystems and American Electronics Association, to the Subcommittee on Economic Policy, Trade and Environment, House Committee on Foreign Affairs (June 9, 1993); Willie Schatz, *Electronic Business* (August 1993), p. 24; "Foreign Availability Review of Computers," U.S. Department of Commerce, Bureau of Export Administration, Office of Foreign Availability (August 28, 1992) (unclassified executive summary).

[18] CISAC interview with Malcolm Wing and Luke Alexander, Sun Microsystems (January 26, 1994).

[19] Although many items do not require pre-approval, Sun must still decipher the difficult-to-read EAR to determine the correct paragraph covering or excluding a certain component from control. Sometimes a product's specifications and manufacturer are difficult to determine as corporate product codes are often incomprehensible. Once Sun tracks down the product's original maker, it often gets little help; a manufacturer will not always know its own part numbers.

[20] U.S. Department of Commerce (April 27, 1993).

[21] EAR, Section 779.1(a), (b) (Technical Data).

[22] Technical data is regulated under the EAR whenever it relates to a controlled commodity, in this case microprocessors. The specific ECCN is 3E01A (from EAR Section 779.2).

[23] There are no published guidelines available for general use when the export of technical data requires a validated export license. Instead, the requirements for any particular export of technical data are determined at the time Commerce approves a license. See EAR, Footnote no. 8 of Section 779.2 (Technical Data).

[24] The exporter must list on the application relevant controlled and proprietary data that it intends to export. Commerce, if it approves the application, may then specify certain conditions and restrictions on the dissemination of that technical data.

[25] Exporters might not always need to receive pre-approval when technical data qualifies under a general license, but an executive officer would probably want to consult with Commerce first to ensure correct understanding. Sun feels that the licensing status of potential exports must be fully clarified to assure legal compliance and to avoid negative publicity.

[26] CISAC interview with Malcolm Wing and Luke Alexander, Sun Microsystems (January 26, 1994).

[27] Personal communications with Luke Alexander, Sun Microsystems (April 7, 1994; February 6, 1995; and March 2, 1995).

[28] To support a project management team of three full-time employees for MCST, Sun spends approximately $450,000 per year. Travel, freight, shipping charges, and customs duties run $100,000 per year. Turbyfill (April 5, 1994). The largest percentage of Sun's costs go to its (proprietary) contracts with MCST, which includes the supply of Sun workstations. On a yearly basis, Sun's investment in MCST is probably equivalent to a few million dollars.

Center for International Security and Arms Control
Stanford University

Please send orders to: Publications, 320 Galvez Street, Stanford, California 94305-6165. Enclose check payable to Stanford University. Add $2.00 postage and handling for first item ordered ($5.00 for overseas delivery), $1.00 for each additional item. California residents, add appropriate sales tax.

Center reports, working papers, and reprints

Herbert L. Abrams and Dan Pollak. *Security Issues in the Handling and Disposition of Fissionable Material.* 1993. (27 pages, $5.00).

Gideon Akavia. *Decisive Victory and Correct Doctrine: Cults in French Military Thought Before 1914.* 1993 (94 pages, $12.00).

Assessing Ballistic Missile Proliferation and Its Control. 1991 (181 pages, $14.00; summary $3.00).

David Bernstein, editor. *Defense Industry Restructuring in Russia: Case Studies and Analysis.* 1994 (236 pages, $14.00).

David Bernstein and Jeffrey Lehrer. *Restructuring of Research Institutes in Russia: The Case of the Central Aerohydrodynamic Research Institute.* 1994 (14 pages, $4.00).

George Bunn and Wolfgang K. H. Panofsky. *Arms Control, Compliance, and the Law* (working paper). 1988 (26 pages, $5.00).

George Bunn. *Does the NPT require its non-nuclear-weapon members to permit inspection by the IAEA of nuclear activities that have not been reported to the IAEA?* 1992 (12 pages, $4.00).

General George L. Butler, Major General Anatoli V. Bolyatko, and Scott D. Sagan. *Reducing the Risk of Dangerous Military Activity* 1991 (39 pages, $6.00).

Cooperative Security in Northeast Asia (text in English and Russian) 1993. (17 pages, $4.00).

Richard D. DeLauer. *Defense Resource Allocation in the 1990s: A Rational Approach.* 1990 (25 pages, $8.00).

John Deutch. *Commercializing Technology: What Should DOD Learn from DOE?* (paper prepared for Carnegie Commission on Science, Technology, and Government). 1990 (10 pages, $4.00).

Sidney D. Drell and Thomas H. Johnson. *Technical Trends and Strategic Policy.* 1988 (41 pages, $9.00).

Anthony Fainberg. *Strengthening IAEA Safeguards: Lessons from Iraq.* 1993 (64 pages, $6.00).

Alexander L. George, David M. Bernstein, Gregory S. Parnell, and J. Philip Rogers. *Inadvertent War in Europe: Crisis Simulation.* 1985 (80 pages, $10.00).

Eric Hamburg. *Arms Control Verification and the U.S. Constitution* (working paper). 1989 (18 pages, $5.00).

John Harvey and Stefan Michalowski. *Nuclear Weapons Safety and Trident.* 1993 (104 pages, $12.00; summary $2.00).

John Harvey and Annie Lin. *Notes on Trident Nuclear Safety.* 1995 (19 pages, $4.00).

Ji, Guoxing. *Maritime Security Mechanisms for the Asian-Pacific Region.* 1994. (25 pages, $5.00).

George N. Lewis, Sally K. Ride, and John S. Townsend. *A Proposal for a Ban on Nuclear SLCMs of All Ranges.* 1989 (13 pages, $5.00).

John Lewis and Xue Litai. *Military Readiness and the Training of China's Sailors.* 1989 (37 pages, $9.00).

John Lewis and Coit D. Blacker, editors. *Next Steps in the Creation of an Accidental Nuclear War Prevention Center.* 1983 (45 pages, $8.00).

Liu, Huaqiu. *China and the Neutron Bomb.* 1988 (49 pages, $9.00).

Michael May and Roger Avedon. *The Future Role of Civilian Plutonium.* 1994 (22 pages, $6.00).

Michael May and Roger Speed. *The Role of U.S. Nuclear Weapons in Regional Conflicts.* 1994 (24 pages, $5.00).

Michael McFaul, ed. *Can the Russian Military-Industrial Complex Be Privatized?* 1993 (60 pages, $6.00).

Captains Moreland, Ota, and Pan'kov. *Naval Cooperation in the Pacific: Looking to the Future.* 1993. (21 pages, $4.00)

Robert F. Mozley. *Uranium Enrichment and Other Technical Problems Relating to Nuclear Weapons Proliferation.* 1994 (64 pages, $9.00)

Thomas Nash. *Human-Computer Systems in the Military Context* (working paper). 1990 (32 pages, $6.00).

Pan, Zhenqiang. *Seeking a Better Strategic Framework in the Asian-Pacific Area* (working paper). 1989 (25 pages, $5.00).

Wolfgang K. H. Panofsky. *Do We Need Arms Control If Peace Breaks Out?* (lecture). 1990 (9 pages, $4.00).

M. Elisabeth Paté-Cornell and Paul S. Fischbeck. *Bayesian Updating of the Probability of Nuclear Attack* (working paper). 1990 (24 pages, $6.00).

Peace, Security, and Cooperation in the Asian-Pacific Region (conference report). 1989 (105 pages $12.00).

William J. Perry. *Defense Investment: A Strategy for the 1990s.* 1989 (43 pages, $9.00).

William J. Perry. *Soviet Defense Conversion—Problems and Opportunities* (testimony) 1992. (7 pages $2.00).

Theodore A. Postol. *Possible Fatalities from Superfires Following Nuclear Attacks in or near Urban Areas* (reprint). 1986 (57 pages, $3.00).

A Program for Strengthening Security and Reducing the Risk of War in the Asian-Pacific Region (text in English and Russian). 1988 (20 pages, $5.00).

Scott D. Sagan, ed. *Civil-Military Relations and Nuclear Weapons.* 1994 (163 pages, $12.00).

Scott D. Sagan and Benjamin A. Valentino. *Nuclear Weapons Safety After the Cold War* (text in English and Russian). 1994 (25 pages, $5.00).

Mark Sakitt. *Submarine Warfare in the Arctic: Option or Illusion?* 1988 (93 pages, $12.00).

Capt. Alexander Skaridov, Cmdr. Daniel Thompson, and Lieut. Cmdr. Yang Zhiqun. *Asian-Pacific Maritime Security: New Possibilities for Naval Cooperation?* 1994 (28 pages, $5.00).

Song, Jiuguang. *START and China's Policy on Nuclear Weapons and Disarmament in the 1990s* . (1991, 29 pages, $5.00).

Konstantin Sorokin. *Russia's Security in a Rapidly Changing World.* 1994. (95 pages, $10.00).

Roger D. Speed. *The International Control of Nuclear Weapons.* 1994 (59 pages, $11.00).

The Transformation of the Asian-Pacific Region: Prospects for the 1990s (conference report) 1991 (191 pages, $15.00).

Selected books available from other publishers

Herbert L. Abrams. *The President Has Been Shot: Confusion, Disability, and the 25th Amendment in the Aftermath of the Assassination Attempt on Ronald Reagan.* New York: W.W. Norton, 1992.

Coit D. Blacker. *Hostage to Revolution: Gorbachev and Soviet Security Policy.* New York: Council on Foreign Relations, 1993.

Coit D. Blacker and Gloria Duffy, editors. *International Arms Control: Issues and Agreements.* Second edition. Studies in International Security and Arms Control. Stanford: Stanford University Press, 1984.

George Bunn. *Arms Control by Committee: Managing Negotiations with the Russians.* Studies in International Security and Arms Control. Stanford: Stanford University Press, 1992.

Gordon H. Chang. *Friends and Enemies: The United States, China, and the Soviet Union, 1948–1972*. Stanford: Stanford University Press, 1990.

Compliance and the Future of Arms Control. Report of a project sponsored by the Center for International Security and Arms Control and Global Outlook, Gloria Duffy, project director. Cambridge: Ballinger Publishing Company, 1988.

Sidney D. Drell. *Facing the Threat of Nuclear Weapons*. Revised edition. Seattle: University of Washington Press, 1989.

Lynn Eden and Steven E. Miller, editors. *Nuclear Arguments: Understanding the Strategic Nuclear Arms and Arms Control Debates*. Ithaca: Cornell University Press, 1989.

Sergei Goncharov, John W. Lewis, and Xue Litai. *Uncertain Partners: Stalin, Mao, and the Korean War*. Stanford: Stanford University Press, 1993.

Robert Hamerton-Kelly. *The Gospel and the Sacred: The Poetics of Violence in the Gospel of Mark*. Fortress Press, 1994.

David Holloway. *Stalin and the Bomb: The Soviet Union and Atomic Energy, 1939-1956*. New Haven: Yale University Press, 1994.

Ryukichi Imai and Henry S. Rowen. *Nuclear Energy and Nuclear Proliferation: Japanese and American Views*. Boulder: Westview Press, 1980.

John Wilson Lewis and Xue Litai. *China Builds the Bomb*. Studies in International Security and Arms Control. Stanford: Stanford University Press, 1988.

John Wilson Lewis and Xue Litai. *China's Strategic Seapower: The Politics of Force Modernization in the Nuclear Age*. Studies in International Security and Arms Control. Stanford: Stanford University Press, 1994.

Michael McFaul, *Post-Communist Politics: Democratic Prospects in Russia and Eastern Europe*. Washington, DC: CSIS, 1993.

Michael McFaul and Sergei Markov, *The Troubled Birth of Russian Democracy: Parties, Personalities, and Programs*. Stanford: Hoover Press, 1993.

A. F. Mullins, Jr. *Born Arming: Development and Military Power in New States*. Studies in International Security and Arms Control. Stanford: Stanford University Press, 1987.

Scott D. Sagan, *Moving Targets: Nuclear Strategy and National Security*. Princeton: Princeton University Press, 1989.

Scott D. Sagan, *The Limits of Safety: Organizations, Accidents, and Nuclear Weapons*. Princeton: Princeton University Press, 1993.